W. J. Schaldach

GENE HILL and STEVE SMITH

The Whispering Wings of Autumn ———

Art by William J. Schaldach

Published by Wilderness Adventures Press™
P.O. Box 1410
Bozeman, MT 59771

10 9 8 7 6 5 4 3

Printed in the United States of America

Third Edition ISBN 1-885106-00-9
Limited Edition of 325   ISBN 1-885106-01-7

First printing (Limited Edition of 1,000), December, 1981
Second printing (Trade Edition), March, 1982
Third printing, September, 1994

For Sue
Typist, partner, friend, wife, who has, for
fourteen autumns, raised the kids with no
visible paternal aid.

Contents

Preface

The grouse and woodcock hunter of today has taken the simple pleasures of hunting and refined them to nearly an art form.

He, or she, has found by habit and design that he has come to fit a mold. And, whether he favors grouse over 'cock, or 'cock above grouse matters little—the mold has produced its proper form, and we live and revel in this casting of our sporting lives.

What of this mold, this simple, functional conformity? The grouse and woodcock hunter tends to carry fine side-by-side 20's, or maybe a slim-wristed little 28. He wears a light vest, usually carries a compass to show him his way home, and has that one certain partner with whom he shares the secrets of the autumn.

The woodcock and grouse specialist is also a creature of secrecy. He has been known to hide his car when working a favorite cover, is as tight lipped as an espionage agent about where the birds are moving, and has taken the time to give all his pet covers a pet name. Talk to such a hunter, and ask him where he is finding birds, and your ears may be assailed by references to "Horseback," the "Old Cabin Cover," the "Forgotten Orchard," or "Custer's Last Stand." He knows these places as intimately as he knows the rooms of his house, and he knows every corner of each where the birds might be.

The best upland partner is one with a terrible memory. He can remember that double you made last season, but will forget the string of eight misses which preceded it. He will remember the point your pup made on his first hunt, but will kindly forget the dozen birds she busted right after that. Mostly, the partner's memory fails when some other hunter asks directions to your favorite haunts.

Not all shooters are as trustworthy as this, however. Most seekers know that a cover can stand only so much shooting. Some men limit their shooting to a certain number of birds taken, shots taken, or visits during the year. Woe be to the loudmouth who wants to show off his knowledge by taking a casual acquaintance to one of your covers on the days when cruel fate dictates you stay at home. This is why two men can keep a secret better than three. My upland partner, Mark Sutton, claims that a third party that hunted with us occasionally for a season went back to our covers with his friends and bespoiled the place. Maybe so. In any event, a grouse and woodcock specialist is likely to look upon a cover as a man would view his new bride—"nobody should touch her but me." Even once is too much.

Watch a man pull up to a favorite cover and find another vehicle in his accustomed place, and you will see the epitome of apoplexy. A thousand thoughts run through his mind. Maybe the other man is just running his dog, maybe he's a rabbit hunter. But, if the interloper emerges from the cover with a little Purdey double and a blooded setter, and his game bag has just a slight bulge in it, you can bet that our man will cross that cover off his operations list. Two parties of such specialists working the same area is one party too many.

Above all, the grouse and woodcock man is a sportsman. Most that I know shoot only over points, usually are happy to quit with a bag lower than the legal limit, and would sooner lose a finger off their shooting hand than lose a dead bird. They realize that shooting is a factor in mortality, especially woodcock, and do their powder burning judiciously and sparingly, knowing that there will be other days, and other seasons.

Our specialist is also a naturalist. Ask a pheasant hunter where the creek is, and he's likely to tell you, "Right over there near that brush." Ask a woodcock hunter or a grouser the same question, and he'll tell you something like, "Right there, next to the speckled alder and that patch of second growth quaking aspen." Knowing the surroundings is part of the game, and the dedicated shooter should take the time to learn such things—it fills out a day even more completely.

But, all is not sweetness and light. The woodcock and grouse shooter has learned that birds, in the long run, cost a lot in time and in money. How many of us have not wished for the time to follow woodcock from New Brunswick to the Carolinas, accompanied by an entourage consisting of blooded pointers, manservants, and cases of smokey colored whiskey? Some men have the wherewithal to do just that and do it.

Others quickly learn that the financial outlay can quickly reach proportions resembling the national debt by just staying around home.

For example, the rabbit hunter may pick up an occasional 'cock, as does the pheasant hunter if he cuts through a brushy woodlot. But the grouse and woodcock hunter usually has a variety of gadgets and paraphernalia for every occasion, and what seems like such an enjoyable pasttime becomes damned expensive in a hurry.

Pump guns or autoloaders give way to feather-light doubles. Soon a second is added with slightly tighter chokes for later in the season when shots are longer. The family car is traded in on a station wagon or a four-wheel-drive vehicle. Dogs come and go, the true 'cock and grouse man may even prefer to hunt behind a brace of matched animals. Sometimes a Lab is kept whose only purpose is to fetch the downed birds. Days away from work are factored in, as well as money for gas, motels, meals out, shells, clothing that makes the wearer appear more or less civilized, and the price jumps still further. On the average, the well-equipped grouse and woodcock hunter will find that his meat totals out at something over $850 a pound. Does this matter? Not a bit, for where these birds are concerned, reason is of little use, and in fact tends to get in the way.

Grouse and woodcock are discussed usually together, because they are found usually together. The grouse is the favorite of most, with the woodcock a dividend. In reality, many professed grouse hunters are really more closet woodcockers than they'd care to admit. If a person says he bagged 20 birds in a season's gunning, ask for particulars. The final count was probably something like 16 woodcock, and four grouse, yet he may call himself a grouse hunter.

As we'll hopefully see in this book, there is nothing wrong with being a woodcock hunter. In fact, there are those who seek the woodcock almost exclusively, taking the grouse as opportunity arises, but seeking woodcock, and grouse hunters that reverse the process. These two birds are, however, like butter-'n-eggs, strawberries and cream, and Hansel and Gretel. In a word, inseparable. I acknowledge the grouse his crown, and do my share of worshipping at the altar of October. But, I also love the woodcock, the bird of mystery. Together, they make up the greatest gunning found anywhere on earth.

Steve Smith

Introduction

It's obvious to those few of you who have followed my writing over the past years, that I take an uncommon interest in the pursuit of woodcock and grouse. I use the word "pursuit" as opposed to "gun" or "hunt" since it is by far the most apt. The word *gun* has always implied, to me anyway, the expenditure of more than two or three boxes of shells a season and to *hunt* carries an image of some rugged and demonic individual ceaselessly trudging through alders and abandoned orchards with his shotgun at port arms and his eyes alert to the possibility of flight from even the least promising of covers.

Typical of my adventures is that for years I have trekked to New Brunswick to stay with my old outfitter-friend, Fred Webb. The covers here are picture-book: stand after stand of alder and birch hard by slightly damp grazing grounds. You'd surely drive by and say to yourself, "These hillsides just have to be stiff with woodcock in the flight season." And you'd be correct, providing you picked the week just after I left to be there. The week after I leave is generally a good time to be anywhere if you're a bird hunter or a salmon fisherman, but especially in New Brunswick. It so happens that the Tobique Valley is one of my absolute favorite places to spend a week or so and if I continue to go back, as I fully intend to do, I shall no doubt hit a week where the woodcock and grouse are confused due to Leap Year or a shift in the lunar tides or something and they'll be there in the numbers usually reserved for "just after you left."

But don't be sorry for me. Just a couple of years ago I ran

into ruffed grouse in Manitoba in literally unbelievable supply. In fact I actually got a true, simultaneous rise, double with my full and full, 32-inch-barrel duck gun. Why a F&F duck gun? Why because I was there to hunt ducks and geese, that's why. I honestly hadn't given a thought to the grouse, but I won't bore you about the following year when I also brought along my Cyl. Imp. *and* Cyl. grouse gun.

It had long been one of my fondest dreams to pursue woodcock in England and not long ago the dream came about. I was lucky enough to be in Wales, hard by the Irish Sea, where fine flights of woodcock aren't unknown—and further luckier on this trip to have had two fine shots at the European woodcock (about twice as big as ours) and to bring one down. My elation lasted until the inevitable "just after you left" letter telling me that from one cover alone they flushed over a hundred birds and the guns took forty-three. Not that my lifetime plan necessarily includes a great bag of woodcock, but how sweet it would be to be able to say "a few" when someone asks me if I've ever shot the bird in Britain instead of merely giving the obviously evasive and plain answer "yes."

In all fairness to myself I feel that I can include the same letter, if you'll allow me to let it cover a trip I'd planned to make and then couldn't. I have memories of those from Michigan, Pennsylvania, Vermont, Maine, North and South Carolina, Louisiana, and last but not least, even Texas. Of course, I always seemed to have missed the week of weeks. These letters frequently use the phrase "never in the memory of even the oldtimers have we seen. . . ." Even taken with the usual grains of salt and allowing for forked tongues I am forced to assume that they took as many birds as they usually do.

I wish there were some way to perform a truly scientific experiment: one week when I'm supposed to be there, but can't; one week when I actually am there and the third—the week after I just left—and see if there is any truth to the wide spreading belief that I am my own jinx, Jonah, or the possessor of evil spirits as far as a couple of species of small brown birds are concerned.

I don't for one minute really believe that a bird with important things on its mind like keeping to a travel schedule, getting married, having babies, finding plenty of good things to eat and drink, seeing old friends, etc., etc., really has any idea of where I am at any given time. Yet, the suspicion grows. However, the odd straggler or uninformed one does cross my path now and then—often enough to keep up my interest in nicely grained walnut stocks, and balance points just slightly behind the hinge pin.

If you'll give me the option of changing my mind, I'll admit that I have stated that the perfect woodcock/grouse gun, for me, would be a 20 bore with 28-inch barrels, bored improved cylinder and improved cylinder, or improved and a very light modified; the old Winchester choking of skeet 1 and skeet 2 would be about perfect. A straight grip English stock with close to an inch of cast-off, with the total weight coming in at 6 to 6½ pounds. The one-ounce load of number 8 shot would do me in most circumstances and 9's for woodcock would be fine.

However (and here a most acquisitive glint comes into my eyes) I have a feeling that I'd do just as well if you gave me the same general statistics but changed the bore to a 28. If it were a side-by-side with good steel barrels I think I'd even like a pair of outside hammers, double triggers and all. I know there are loads of arguments waiting in the wings; I'll agree that I'm not a ballistician and be the first to admit to more than my share of failing as a wing shot. *But,* there are guns that do shoot better in the field than the scientific minds say they can on paper: a notable example being the truly magnificent .375 H & H Magnum rifle.

And there is a certain amount of personal experience behind what I say. I have a good friend who lets me shoot his 28 gauge on our annual dove outing and I have totally convinced myself that I do as well with that as I can do with the 20 . . . and I have the annual skeet averages of the top shooters which shows that, give or take a target in a thousand, their 20 and 28 scores are just about the same. (So are mine, by the way, if you need the urge for a good laugh.)

I will mention the .410 just to keep those who are curious

from asking me: I see no place in the field whatever for this gauge—in anybody's hands for any game bird. End of my opinion of the .410.*

   If you ever see me in the upland covers and ask me, "Where's the 28-gauge you're so high on?" I will resist the urge to strangle you and admit that I sold them both when I was in so strange a mood and frame of mind that I can't even remember why. Suffice it to say that I am very, very sorry and know now how quickly and mightily stupidity can strike the best of us when it comes to shotguns. Not that either was close to the legendary "best London gun" but even so, I wish I had them still. (If anyone out there has one, please, for the sake of my sanity, don't write me a letter that says "just last week. . . .")

   Just in passing, I ought to say that I wish the gun laws that require a "waiting period" before you can buy one also applied to a waiting period before you sell. It would make just as much sense as far as the crime rate is concerned, but, more importantly, a lot of us would still own stuff we'll forever regret trading off. Where's good government when you really need it?

   I suppose it's obvious that I spend an irrational amount of time and thought messing around with woodcock, woodcock guns, woodcock this and woodcock that. Of course I do; anyone who has spent as much time as I have in covers so thick you can't throw your hat on the ground is obviously irrational. It's an irrational bird and you have to be on equal terms! What other creature do you know of that was a shore bird not too long ago and said to hell with that and left the sandy beaches and the seaside marsh for perpendicular hillsides and impenetrable alder thickets? It's just another part of the mystery of a bird that is said to carry its young between its legs and has had scores of learned ornithologists arguing for years whether his little peenting whistle is done through his bill or by his wings. What other bird dances in the Spring moonlight just so that

---

* Publisher's Note: Mr. Hill has long been suspected of harboring an unreasonable attitude toward a certain person's uncanny skill with an old Winchester Model 42 (obviously .410!) on both whitewings and mourning doves.

otherwise decent, sane people will stay up half the night just to watch this avian madness? Why won't an otherwise superb retriever pick up one without looking like he wants to spit or use a mouthwash? All do this for the same reason I'm willing and eager to run through the rent and grocery money for a 28 gauge, spend an embarrassing amount of time and trouble driving all over the country to run through six or eight shells and have about half my outdoor library stocked with titles that start with "W."

I'm a dedicated waterfowler, a devotee of pheasant and quail and can hardly wait for September to get into flighting doves. But when you think about it for a minute, you'll agree that, given this or that little circumstance, these are fairly reliable birds. They are, for the most part, where they should be when they should be. They are as rational and as well behaved as a banker; you know their hours and their places of business. When you itch for one of these you can reach where you want to scratch.

But your woodcock is at best a blind date. He promises to meet you at the corner by the best worm restaurant in the county and you get there right on time and where is he? It seems he just forgot or got lost or found another eatery he likes better; no messages, no forwarding address. He's fickle, untrustworthy, unpunctual, selfish and rude. He takes the money I've saved to buy my wife a new washer and makes me toss it away on a new stock with a quarter-inch less drop.

Well, I've learned my lesson. No more listening to promises about October in Canada or November in Maine. No more hanging around waiting in the birches with the running spring. Well, maybe just one more time, come the first full moon before a heavy frost is due, there is *one* section of cover that I've got to visit. But if I do and there's a letter later that says "just after you left. . . ." and I find an alder leaf and a little whitewash in it, I absolutely, positively quit.

Gene Hill

Foreword

When *The Whispering Wings of Autumn* was first published in December of 1981, I was sent a slipcased copy inscribed by both authors. Smith wrote: "For Dave: hunting partner, friend, and a true sportsman—of which there are too few." On the next page, Hill wrote: "Your reward for having to hunt with Steve Smith will be hunting with Gene Hill!"

One very sincere, one wry humor; either author could have written either inscription—and it's happened that way, in other times and other places, in writing and in person. That's the way these two, who I have the privilege of calling friends, are; funny, witty, quick to share a laugh and a smile, but at the same time, knowledgeable, and totally sincere—reverential, if you will—in their passion for the covert, and the birds and dogs and guns of the upland gunner's life.

The range of the writings—and the emotions—contained herein reflect the talent of the authors—hard facts, eye-glazing reflections, and side-splitting humor—all wrapped up in one of the best all-around treatises on grouse and woodcock—especially woodcock—ever produced.

Listen to Hill: "I suppose it's obvious that I spend an irrational amount of time and thought messing around with woodcock, woodcock guns, woodcock this and woodcock that. Of course I do; anyone who has spent as much time as I have in covers so thick you can't throw your hat on the ground is obviously irrational. It's an irrational bird and you have to be on equal terms!"

And Smith on the same subject: "He is, then, a symbol. A symbol of the reclusiveness of the wild, the mysteries of the hunt, and the autumn bounty on this continent. He and his friend the grouse *are* the Whispering Wings of Autumn."

That's Hill and Smith, Smith and Hill; they can't help it, it's the way they are, the set of their minds; holding personally and privately a special kinship with the out-of-doors, yet sharing it freely with those of like mind and ethic.

I've had the privilege of breaking bread and sharing a favorite covert or two with each of them— times I cherish. I pray the good Lord will grant us, again, time together, borne on the Whispering Wings of Autumn.

Dave Meisner
The Pointing Dog Journal
Adel, Iowa

Acknowledgments

I'd like to acknowledge a number of people who made this book possible. In no particular order of importance—because all their contributions were equally important—I'd like to thank the following people:

Dr. James Levinson of Saginaw Valley State College for overseeing my work on woodcock migrations. Jim helped extrapolate the data and kept me going through dead ends with words like, "That's the way it goes—keep plugging."

I'd like to thank Mark Dilts, editor of *The Drummer*, the publication of The Ruffed Grouse Society, for his help and for writing the foreword of this book.

I'd like to thank Dr. Samuel R. Pursglove, Jr., Executive Director of The Ruffed Grouse Society for his help and assistance also, especially in the area of woodcock findings. Sam is no mean expert on the little brown birds.

Certainly, Gordon Gullion of the Univeristy of Minnesota should be thanked for letting me reproduce the management maps contained herein. Gordy, probably the greatest grouse expert presently in captivity, serves tirelessly as chairman of the Projects Committee of the Ruffed Grouse Society, and is the leader of perhaps the most comprehensive grouse study area in the world.

Fins & Feathers magazine, through editor, Gary Warner, also come in for thanks for allowing the reproduction of the woodcock migration maps.

I'd like to thank editor/publisher Jim Rikhoff for helping

and advising on this book and for making things more or less blend smoothly.

Naturally, I'd like to thank Gene Hill for his fine work in the collaboration. He is the best there is, hands down.

Lastly, I'd like to thank two people for their work. First, boyhood buddy Mark Sutton for serving as advisor and confidante these many years, and for following my schemes for locating more grouse and woodcock. As chief dog handler, great shot and fine companion, none is better.

Lastly, my wife Sue who tolerated me through the preparation of the book and typed the finished manuscript comes in for special praise. Without her, it couldn't have been done.

Steve Smith

The Woodcock Letter

Dear Marcia:

I suppose you and the kids have been wondering what happened to me since the night, a week ago, when I went out to get whiskey. And I suppose my office has been bothering you about my absence.

Well, the answer as to where I've been—and still am—is simple, but the reasons why I am here are somewhat hard to follow. So, please be patient and try.

You remember kidding me about having six or eight books on woodcock on my bed table and how it seemed to you I read about practically nothing else? And how you re-marked that the only way I'd get to know more about the bird than I already know would be to talk to one?

Well, as I was going up the lane in the car my headlights picked up a woodcock feeding along the side of the road. He (perhaps she; you'll recall how I told you about the difficulty of telling the sexes apart—and how the female is generally slightly larger and the bill slightly longer . . .) seemed much less shy than I anticipated. So boldened by curiosity, I stopped the car and very slowly and quietly got out of the front seat and walked within a few feet of the bird. He had stopped feeding and was peering at me—his huge soft brown eyes glit-tering like amber diamonds in the reflected light from the car. More for fun than anything else, I went, "peent . . . peent" or at least attempted what I thought a woodcock would sound like. He seemed only slightly astonished that I would make an effort to communicate with him and after only a moment's hesitation, he too went, "peent ... peent."

Now I have never heard of a wild game bird making any effort to communicate with man, but here, clearly, was a creature who understood me. Suddenly I remembered that the little belt can of fish worms was still in the back seat of the car and stealthily I glided around the car to where I could reach down and get it. I picked out a worm and tossed it softly near him. He stepped over and tucked it away as if I'd been feeding him for years.

Clearly we had some sort of understanding going on. My mind raced through several possibilities. Should I try to capture and tame him? Should I see if we could establish some kind of talk right now ... or should I quit this moment and go about my business and let him go on about his? Then he made up my mind for me. Ever since I had given him the worm, he had been staring at me in a rather curious fashion—almost as if he could read my thoughts. He had apparently noticed where the worm had come from and with a few very stately hops he was in the back seat of the car probing busily in my bait can. In a moment or two he had gobbled the contents and seemed full. He regarded me in a rather friendly fashion once more and then seemed to settle himself down in my fishing shirt and looked as though he wished to take a little nap.

I climbed in the car, softly closed the door and started down the driveway—I wasn't really sure where I was going to go but I felt an urgency to move south toward the rising moon.

As the car moved on a few miles, the little fellow in the back seat awoke and hopped up on the dashboard in front of me and watched the proceedings. It wasn't too long until I had a feeling that he understood what was happening. He began to march nervously back and forth over the part of the dash where the clock is and tap his bill on the windshield as though to indicate the direction he wanted us to follow. As soon as I determined this—or thought I had—I began to leave the highway and found myself following a zig-zag series of long neglected country roads. And, as it was when we began, in front of us I could always see the ascending moon. Now and then, the woodcock would give voice to a mild "peent . . . peent." Not so much a call as it was the voicing of a thing well done. He seemed to be saying, "yes . . . yes . . ." as the car veered from one unknown road to another. As we journeyed through the night he seemed alert and cheerful. Someone who knew what he was doing and the best way to get the job done.

However, as the morning sun arose it seemed to depress him. He seemed less sure of our direction and, if not disinterested, at least not terribly concerned. As for myself, I was, as you may have guessed, getting more than a little tired. Finally we got to the point, somewhere near Cape May County, New Jersey, of mutual exhaustion. I pulled the car off the log road we'd been traveling, and fell asleep.

When I awoke it was to the insistent summons of my traveling companion, tapping on the windshield and pacing back and forth, eager to step outside in the gathering dusk. It was with some questioning of myself that I opened the door and watched him flutter past my face into the nearby meadow. But the nonchalance of his exit and the brevity of his flight gave me some reassurance that our acquaintance had taken some deep rooting in the past few hours.

I followed him out and decided that I'd give him a hand and turned-to-rolling over some nearby stones and tossing the earthworms I found in his direction. He accepted them gratefully. After 15 or 20 worms had been swallowed he staggered contentedly toward the car, propped himself back up on the dashboard and signaled me to get moving.

That, in brief, Marcia and my beloved children, is what happened. The events of the first day's journey have been repeated time and again and I suspect we are headed for some spot in Louisiana where he intends to spend the winter. Our conversations have been mutually informative and a deep friendship has developed—far enough so that on more than one day's journey I have had several of his acquaintances traveling with us. Those too old or tired, from the looks of them, to do it all alone on wing.

I must apologize for the undue worry and concern I have caused you all at home and in the office; but I trust you understand the uniqueness of my journey. And, if you do not fully comprehend how I feel about it, I know that you are at least sympathetic to my emotions.

Trusting all is well, I again apologize. We are nearing the end of our journey and I believe I will be able to start homeward in less than a week from today.

My love to all,
Gene

Woodcock–The Upland Prince

Throughout much of North America each autumn, a strange ritual is carried out by a small, but dedicated group of hunters and outdoorsmen. These people are woodcock hunters, probably the most select band of shooters that ever raised a smoothbore or licked a wrist scratched from the clutching thorns.

The reason so few seek him, is because the American woodcock (*Philohela minor*) lives in some awful places, flies like a windblown oak leaf, and—to some—represents a tiny morsel of protein. Far better, some feel, to expend that time, energy, and gunpowder on something like a pheasant, grouse, or goose which will feed the family and fill the freezer with but a minimum outlay of energy.

But the true woodcock hunter, the man who seeks these birds to the exclusion of all others, takes part in a spectacle as old as man himself—the hunt. For most of us, hunting brings to mind the cascading leaves of autumn, the brilliant maples, the golden aspen, and the flaming sumac. With most birds, however, this is not the case. Speak of pheasants, and the hunter envisions browned and leaning cornstalks. The grouse hunter admires the colorful landscape, but knows his sport will improve when cold weather removes the screening foliage, and secretly hopes for this to happen. The duck or goose hunter really finds his best sport when the weather is too mis-

erable for even these birds to fly, and he yearns for a leaden
sky, with just a touch of snow and a howling nor'wester

Not so the woodcock hunter. The season of flaming color
is his season of the year. Those of us who know this bird know
that the colors bring us action and enjoyment. We also know
that when these colors have faded and fallen, our little friends
will have moved on, leaving the covers as drab as the landscape, and we must wait another year for that magic period
when they again muster their forces for the trip south. Our
employers cast a wistful eye at the calendar; we'll get little
work done while the season of the woodcock is upon us.

The woodcock, you see, is the essence of autumn. He is
the fall colors, bluebird days, and wind-blown cumulus clouds
all rolled together. He is a fine pointing dog, a fine double-gun,
and leather-topped, rubber-bottomed boots. He is the incar-
nate form of all that is good and plentiful on this continent. He
is opportunity and mystery.

If he is all these things, what of the men who seek him in
his out of the way haunts? The typical woodcock hunter lives
for those few weeks when the birds are on the move, prepar-
ing for the movement south. He is given to spasms of ecstasy
when his gun operates like an extension of his eyesight, and
his dog works as if he is controlled by the hunter's very mind.
He is gloomy and inconsolable if his work schedule means he
has to miss the mystical "flights," and he lives in a dream
world when his covers are alive with these tawny migrants.

As you may have gathered by now, there is a tendency
among such gunners to engage in a bit of snobbery about their
favorite sport. This is to be expected. Every upland gunner is
guilty of this when discussing his favorite quarry, and woodcock shooters are just as big at the holier-than-thou routine as
the grouse specialist or a ducking man and his blacks.

However, with woodcock hunters, it goes deeper. He
tends to view the grouser who takes an occasional 'cock as an
interloper, a usurper of the worst kind. He seems to feel that
nobody has a right to take a woodcock save himself, because
nobody will truly appreciate the bird except the man who

ventures forth to risk scratches and falls solely for the purpose of shooting a few woodcock.

Frankly, a true woodcock devotee looks upon the happenstance woodcock harvester the way one might view the ugly man who marries his beautiful sister and then stays out all night drinking: damned lucky and undeserving.

Besides this, there is a certain snobbery associated with being able to talk intelligently about a bird most people don't even realize exists, and certainly competition for the bird is minimal. In Michigan, which leads the nation in woodcock kills, if I had to count the number of true woodcock hunters I know, I'd be stuck thinking of more after I assembled enough for a good bridge game. What's more, we like it that way.

And, my friend, what of the bird itself? The woodcock is often thought of as being a most peculiar bird, put together from the spare parts left over when the rest of the birds were made by that great Bird Maker. But the woodcock is actually a perfect example of evolutionary adaptation.

For every strange, to us, bit of machinery in his little carcass, or for every "strange" behavior, there is a reason, one which appears to perfectly keep this bird in tune with its environment and ensure its longevity as a species.

For example, the bird sees better at night and at dusk and dawn because that is when he is most active, preferring to feed at the twilight hours. He even courts and mates under the stars, his peculiar sky dancing courtship ritual being a true harbinger of spring.

The hen nests on the ground, but her coloration is so perfect that few nests are lost to predators. The little hen is brave enough to withstand handling in some cases, and the survival rate among the chicks is almost phenomenal, sometimes as high as nearly two young for every adult hen before the autumn migrations begin.

That long bill is perfectly constructed for probing, sensing and latching onto the worms and other invertebrates that he relishes so much, and the ears are even located at the base of the bill to aid in sensing underground movement.

The high-set eyes allow him to keep his bill in the ground and still see danger approaching, and his upside down brain has been pushed there by evolutionary forces that forced the cerebellum up high where it had more room to develop. This part of the brain controls the motor, or voluntary muscles, which means the bird has total control when flying. There is nothing clumsy about friend woodcock. Where a grouse may hammer through small branches upon flushing, the large cerebellum allows the woodcock to simply twitter around them.

His heart, huge in comparison to his body size, gives him the vital blood flow that helps in long flights during migration. The fact that he flies much and walks little makes his breast meat dark and his legs and thighs white. Dark meat means a preponderance of blood vessels, so it's easy to see which a bird does the most of by examining the color of the meat—flying or legging it.

He is a shorebird that has found things more to his liking in the uplands, but again this shows his adaptability as a species. As glacial pools dried after melting, the bird moved into the uplands. One of the precepts of science says that an animal either changes with condition—structurally or behaviorally—or dies as a species. The woodcock can change. In fact, he is usually one of the first creatures to come back when an old farm starts to return to the wild upon abandonment. He knows a good thing when he sees it. And, when cattle are pastured nearby, he will use the soil richened by their droppings as a place to probe for food.

His metabolism, like all birds, is fast. This means he never gets too weighted down to fly. The droppings, called "whitewash" are a true indication of his presence, for you'll see very few old whitewashings, dew and frost or even light drizzle conspiring to remove the telltale sign. This means that if you find whitewash, it was made no earlier, usually, than the previous night.

Because of all these adaptations, the woodcock is quite well suited to live out his life in peace and solitude, knowing few enemies. In fact, outside of the orange-clad men who seek him, and ornithologists, most people don't even know him by sight, and definitely few can pick him out of a bird field guide by name only.

Being migratory in nature, he usually leaves before things get tough, and if he doesn't, he dies—nature's way of weeding out the idiots. The strain is cleansed. The housecat is his biggest enemy, proof that man can tamper with the habitat and ecosystem by adding an "unnatural" predator.

Luckily, and I say this sincerely, hunting is really a major source of predation on woodcock. Luckily, because you can't legislate against weather. No fox, hawk or owl follows the season and bag limits, but hunting can be controlled. If things look thin, shorten the limits or the season. As it is, the woodcock is probably underharvested as a game bird, less than two million bagged in any given year, compared to that many doves in each of several states. I compare the dove because he is mostly migratory, but in the Great Lakes states, more and more are sticking around the whole winter. Not the woodcock—he knows better.

Another factor which controls the woodcock mortality is the ineptitude of the average scattergunner when it comes to bagging these birds. They fly in a manner that defies description. They twitter, twist, and fly like moths or wind blown leaves. None of these describe the flight accurately. They simply fly like woodcock, their wings whistling a goodbye to you, and a hello to autumn.

I have no use for the gunners who think it fine to shoot over the limit because others choose not to hunt the bird. More hunters should recognize the use of bag limits. If biologists expected every hunter to get the limit every day out, the limit would easily be halved immediately. To take the limit every time is unthinkable to the true 'cock hunter, even if possible. As more birds are taken, each ceases to be an individual happening, and is harder to recall in pleasant memory. Most of my boyhood days were days of one, maybe two 'cock, fairly taken, with real affection for the birds I'd shot.

Even on the table he is an enigma. Woodcock either tickle your palate, or cause you to look for the closest potted palm. They are either your culinary *pièce de resistance,* or canned dog food, for there is no middle of the road with 'cock. Like spinach, gale force winter winds, and FDR, you either love him or hate him.

Some epicures prefer to eat the birds European style, with the entrails intact. I do not choose to carry a good thing to its final degree so that I may revel in the absurd. No, I like my birds with feathers off and inside out—with a strip of bacon, if you please, and make the toast golden brown, as brown as the bourbon I nurse before dinner. A robust wine to top it off, and I can only pity those who pass him up at table.

But in a sense, his taste is another defense mechanism. Imagine what the continental population of birds would be if all woodcock shooters felt as you and I? With the forces of heavy gunning clutching at him from every angle, we may have to put up with shorter seasons and fewer birds. So, let others eat goose and gravy, quail and dumplings. You and I will enjoy, in privacy, the greatest thrill in the uplands—woodcock hunting and eating!

The woodcock is actually far more popular than you may think. The thing is, nobody feels like admitting they are woodcock hunters. It is so much more glamorous to claim you are shooting grouse. A season ago, I saw three men hunting a marginal grouse cover. I stopped my four-wheel-drive as they emerged, and asked about their luck.

"Not much, just a few woodcock," was the reply. I offered congratulations, not condolences, and the crowd brightened. It turns out that they concentrate on woodcock, taking the odd grouse by chance. When they found out I was often of the same cut, they were relieved and relaxed, and we talked woodcock for a quarter of an hour. It seems the woodcock hunter is as strange as his quarry in ways.

Many others still steadfastly claim they are grouse hunters, but make trips in the early season only, not later. If they were after grouse, why not go more later on when cover is thinned by the weather? The answer is they are after woodcock, and when the birds are gone, so is their interest.

Part of the allure of the woodcock is the fact that he is an early season target. As the gunner seeks him, his thoughts may fly ahead to grouse, quail, ducks, pheasant, and even deer and rabbits. I know, for example, that I'll have a lot of company on that first weekend or two, but most will be there on a passing whim. A chance to get out, shoot the old gun, and see the dog work is what these men seek. Many of my acquaintance think of the woodcock as I view the crow—a target of opportunity on which to sharpen skills for the later, more "crucial" tests.

But for some, the woodcock is the end-all. It is with him in mind that we watch for the first leaves to color, get up early to look for that first frost, and observe the geologic structure of rivers and valleys. Perhaps it is he that is sought above all others. He is our glamour boy, our link with the past when woodcock were the sought-after prize of prizes, and the shooting started on the Fourth of July.

He is, then, a symbol. A symbol of the reclusiveness of the wild, the mysteries of the hunt and the autumn bounty on this continent. He and his friend the grouse are the Wings of Autumn.

Steve Smith

Woodcock Habits and Habitat

The woodcock leads a relatively sedate life, compared to some. He is not overly preyed upon, lives out his days in relative obscurity compared to more glamorous species, and is unknown throughout much of his home range.

However, more is being learned each year, much is still mystery, and much more needs to be done.

We can, however, comment on the basics of his lifestyle. The purpose of this book is not to act as a scientific treatise on the life of the American Woodcock. Other, more scholarly works do a better job of it, and are devoted to his natural history almost entirely.

Instead, what I'd like to do is give some of the high points of his life cycle, seasonal cycles, and daily habits for the hunter, so that enjoyment can be expanded throughout the year.

First off, the woodcock's year begins in spring, when the birds return from the wintering grounds, prompted by the inner drive to procreate. They will arrive in the North country—New England, the Great Lakes, and the Maritimes, usually just as the snow is coming off the ground. Courtship has taken place along the way, and mating may occur then as well, but they really get serious about the whole thing when they reach their own turf, the place that genetic imprinting tells them is home.

The males court the females with a variety of songs, and

insect-like buzzing, which finally culminates in the famous sky-dancing exhibition, when the males fly into a spiral into the gathering dark of an early spring evening, singing the most beautiful song I've ever heard come from the bill of a bird.

These singing grounds are used year after year as long as vegetation stays down, such as on recently abandoned farm fields.

Sometimes, the grounds are used by succeeding generations of 'cock for years. The male courts, the female listens and comes when she is ready, and copulation occurs.

Shortly afterward, the hen builds a simple nest on the ground in what could be called typical woodcock resting cover—ferns and second-growth aspen mixed with alders. The male becomes a bachelor again, hanging around the swamps bragging to his buddies about his conquests. The hen broods the eggs—usually four—until they hatch the cutest little fluffs you'll ever lay eyes on.

Typically, the young have a high survival rate, and Momma Woodcock dotes on her babes. This family arrangement is probably why the males migrate later in autumn than the females and young, when the weather could sneak in a knockout punch. Males are excess baggage to the woodcock population, and it is the females and young that migrate south the earliest in the fall when conditions are right and comfortable.

The young grow quickly, and by four weeks can fly, and the family group breaks up. This process will be repeated for generations, provided care is exercised.

For the sportsman, the spring dance is the time when he can get a firsthand look at who's returning from the South, and a chance to be out witnessing one of the wild displays of nature. In fact, I often hear the spring song in the early evening while trudging back to my car after a day of trout fishing. Perhaps it is wrong, but I always mentally jot down the location, planning to return in the fall with my shotgun. I seldom do, probably being too softhearted.

In the summer, the woodcock goes about his daily habits in a regimented manner. Twilight finds him in his resting covers, awaiting the sun's demise. When things get so you'll need your headlights, you'll often see the woodcock flitting before the lights as they head for feeding cover. They will feed with a hearty appetite until dawn, not constantly, but within the cover.

As dawn comes up, and first light cuts the inky sky, they return to the resting cover to relax, dust, and kibitz until the procedure is repeated again. Thus will it remain while the young grow, the adults rest up for the coming migration, and the species exists in tranquility.

For the hunter, it is fun in the summer to try "lining" the flight of these dusking woodcock, either morning or evening. It is a good way to locate covers, gives you an idea of the local population, and helps you find how productive an area is. For example, if you see woodcock going into a feeding cover from three directions, you'll know the population is scattered, not concentrated, and that hunting will produce birds few and far between. If, however, the birds are going to a feeding cover from one direction, it is simple to backtrack the flight—take lining a bee tree—to locate one great resting cover. All of this assumes, of course, that no cover will be overshot or over-hunted once the season opens.

Locating covers this way is a fine method for the shooter to set up his circuit of covers. Most woodcock hunts consist of the hunting of several covers in a day, and these rightfully should be rested for a few days between visits. It is not un-common for most shooters to have so many covers that they visit each one no more than twice in a given shooting season. This, of course, makes for more sporting shooting, and doesn't damage populations.

If you observe birds moving, or dusking in an area, here is where the government can do something for you. Get hold of several topographical maps from the U.S. Geologic Survey in 7½ minute configuration and look them over in the area of interest. The land formations will probably indicate to you where the birds are coming from, or if you see them leave a resting cover, the maps will help you locate the feeding cover.

More shooters annually are turning to woodcock, and this

is especially evident when the grouse cycle turns down throughout woodcock range. For this reason, shooters should get to know the birds and their habits better.

Part of getting to know the birds better is being able to identify the game in hand by sex and age. This is part of knowing the bird, keeping track of the movements, and also in determining the productivity of the nesting season.

It is not nearly as hard as you'd think. First of all, sex: The female is overall a chunkier, heavier bird than the male, and the bill is longer. This works just dandy if you've got one of each sex in hand, but otherwise, you'll need a measuring stick, so pick up the kind that is gauged in metrics. The top bills of almost all males will be 66 millimeters or shorter. The shortest I ever measured was 57mm, and this was unusual.

The top bill of the female will be longer, from 77mm down to around 67mm. There is, however, a gray area in which a long male bill or a short female bill can be confusing, say when the bill is around 67 or 68mm. A millimeter is tiny, and it is easy to get a bit mixed up when measuring, so the use of the wing is by far the most effective method of determining sex.

To find sex with the wing, locate and isolate the first primary flight feather of either wing. Measure down from the outer tip 2 centimeters and measure the width at this point. The female's feather will be a shade under 4mm, and the male a shade under three.

As long as you've got the wing pulled out, you may as well check the age of the bird. Locate the secondary flight feathers. These lie in layers atop the stiffer primaries. Pick out one in the middle of the row and examine the color pattern. An immature bird will have well defined buff and dark brown bands on the tip of this feather, the adult will have a more mottled appearing feather.

The U.S. Office of Migratory Bird Management in Laurel, Maryland, makes great use of the wings sent in by shooters to make judgments and compile data on the bird, in the hope of clearing up some of the mysteries shrouding this elusive creature.

In any event, I think the hunter owes it to the bird to learn as much as he can about it, and sexing and aging are part of it. It takes away nothing from the charm of a bird in hand, and in fact makes it more of an individual to me. Try it.

By the way, as part of respect for the bird, and for the sake of accuracy, I call woodcock just that: woodcock. I detest "timberdoodle, bogsucker, wood snipe" and all the other local names. For the same reason, grouse are grouse, not "pats, partridge, mountain pheasants or thunderbirds." A little pet peeve, perhaps, but woodcock and grouse are the best names to describe these birds. Oh, yes, a female woodcock is not a woodhen—she's a female woodcock.

Steve Smith

Predicting Woodcock Migration

For generations, the mystery of what makes woodcock migrate has been kept hidden from the shooter by the bird's whimsical nature—here today, gone the next. Certainly, a woodcock hunter's success and enjoyment could be enhanced greatly if he had some sort of guarantee that he was working productive covers.

Weather conditions, naturally, affect woodcock in their migration like other creatures, but it takes a very special set of weather conditions to make the birds migrate.

The legendary "flights," in which the birds suddenly populate a cover in staggering numbers are really a rarity, happening so seldom that flight gunning is almost unheard of by experienced shooters. When it does happen, it is a time for rejoicing.

However, the most productive shooting comes when the birds migrate slowly, but steadily. This 'trickling through' of birds puts two or three in a cover where there were none the day before, or replaces the two that were carried out of that same cover in the lucky shooter's game bag the day before.

In truth, the sport lasts longer this way, because large flights, pushed downward from the north, have a tendency to end the shooting for the year. The sportsman would rather have longer, more sustained shooting rather than a day or two of wild activity followed by weeks of empty covers.

How, then, can a shooter predict when the migration is underway, and how can he know when and where to plan his forays for this elusive little bird?

Most shooters wrongly assume that migration takes place just as winter is about to slam shut the door on the fall season. Part of this stems from the fact that too few people are in the covers before the season opens, and don't see that woodcock may already be moving south. The birds they find during the first days of the open season are thought to be natives, or birds which have spent the nesting season in that locale. These birds may be the first of the hordes of tawny migrants, poised to head toward the wintering grounds in the Deep South.

Woodcock tend to migrate as individuals, not as flocks like geese. If you find three birds in a cover that yesterday held none, it is because that cover looked good to three separate birds during the night before, when woodcock migrate. Because of this, the factors affecting each bird are multiplied by the number of birds found in a cover: three birds, then, means three separate migrations.

Whenever the habits of a wild creature are discussed, the overriding consideration that biologists use is: "Of what benefit is this behavior to the bird, animal, plant or other organism?" Bearing this in mind, we know that woodcock are partial to streams because the moist earth near the streambed is a source of food. Being lower and more damp than the surrounding landscape, the streambeds do not freeze as rapidly as higher elevations, and hold the worms, grubs and other invertebrates that the woodcock relishes.

But in addition to this, the birds use the streambeds as navigational aids. Every river in woodcock country will lead, eventually, to a larger river that runs south, a line of hills or glacial moraines that run somewhat south, or to a shore of the great lakes, which will be used to guide the birds southward to the wintering grounds.

Given this, what is the prime weather condition that will

cause the birds to migrate in the "trickle through" described earlier? Wind. Not the cold, blustery winds of a late autumn cold front, for these result in the rarely seen "Flights," but instead, the breeze which will serve as a tailwind for this small, light bird as it moves down its chosen streambed to larger streams or land formations which will influence the bird to move south.

For example, if river A flows straight south, and stream B meets river A, entering from the west, then a westerly wind will move the birds living on stream B toward the river. The gunner, then, will find his covers along stream B alive with birds the night after a westerly wind blew. Where B joins A, birds will congregate.

If, on that same river system, another stream—we'll call it C—entered from the east, then an east wind would become a tailwind for these birds, but would be a headwind for the birds moving along stream B. Therefore, the thoughtful gunner will hunt in covers along stream C the day after an evening easterly wind came up.

For the sake of argument, let's say that a little feeder creek entered the westerly flowing stream C from the south, this would be the migration pattern for birds living there: south wind, move from the feeder creek to stream C. East wind, move to the south-flowing river. North wind, head south.

Witness the example of Cape May, New Jersey. Here, the birds must wait for a tailwind to carry them across the vast expanses of Delaware Bay. A headwind, and the birds will wait.

Besides wind, the other factor appears to be the use of the stars to guide the birds in their migrational paths, much like early seamen used the stars for navigation. Biologists call this "celestial navigation," and latest studies indicate that nocturnal migrators such as woodcock use the stars a great deal.

Clear skies, then, are a great aid to the migrating woodcock, because they can then use the stars as a further guide. With these two factors, then, the woodcock hunter can get a good idea of how to predict migration. The first thing to real-

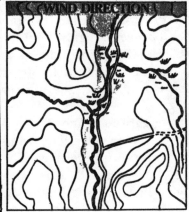

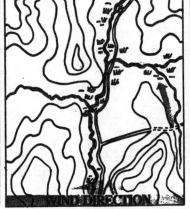

NORTH *wind gets birds moving all along main north-south stream. Make for marshy ground and hunt in the shelter cover near feed grounds.*

SOUTH *wind halts birds on main stream. If you already know where they are, hunt there, but best bet is north-south creek that later joins main stream.*

How Will Wind Affect Woodcock?

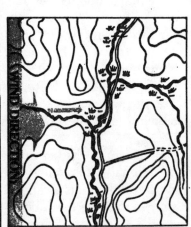

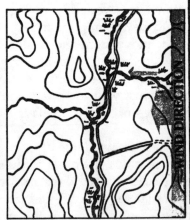

WEST *wind moves woodcock east toward main north-south stream where they join southbound migration. If there's marsh where streams meet, hunt nearby.*

EAST *wind does the opposite. birds move westward to join main north-south migration route. Use topo map to locate likely streams with marshy shorelines.*

ize is that your average woodcock is not going to be caught in the northern climes when the ground freezes hard. They are going to start looking for the chance to migrate when decreasing amounts of sunlight—shorter days—triggers the urge in them to be gone. In northern New England, Michigan, Wisconsin, and Minnesota, this is on or about October first— much earlier than most hunters suspect.

After that time, the shooter should pick out his favorite stream or system of streams, and watch the weather report. If he finds that the prediction calls for westerly winds and clear skies, he should plan to hunt, the next day, the banks and valley covers of a stream that flows from the west to a larger river valley which runs south, or mostly south.

If the local weatherman calls for north winds, he should hunt the main river's valley. If the report says south winds, he should be prepared to find a small feeder creek or stream which meanders from the south to join with a larger stream which will eventually flow into a north/south river.

My studies indicate that cold weather has little effect on early migration. In fact, the birds migrated less when the temperatures were under 32 degrees than when warmer night temperatures were recorded. Rain, and even snow, tends to slow down migration because the birds cannot use the stars to find their way. Besides, rain and snow means low pressure air, hard for any bird to fly through because their wings have to work harder to make headway. The worst times for migration appear to be when a low pressure air mass hovers over the covers. The birds stay put, not wanting to move. This can be helpful if the birds were in your covers in good numbers, because it means they'll stay put. When the skies clear, however, they'll be gone with the first favorable winds.

A lot has been written about how the woodcock need such nice weather or they'll be absent. To a great extent this is true, but in the Great Lakes region, the birds often come back to their nesting grounds before the spring snows are gone and every self-respecting worm in the state is below the frost line. Don't be fooled into thinking the birds will be gone for the year during the gunning season if the weather conjures up a late fall snow squall. When this happens, they just ride it out and wait for the favorable conditions to take their leave. Cold bothers the birds, no doubt, but headwinds are the real menace to them, and the little six-ounce rusty brown fellows will simply refuse to fight them.

The migration prediction sword, however, can cut two ways. If the covers were full of birds today, a favorable wind and clear skies can take these birds away, and may not replace them with others for several days. Likewise, a south wind will stop most migration in north/south valleys, and thus keep the birds around for several days.

One day a few seasons back, my gunning partner and I were struggling hard to find birds, but their usual haunts produced nearly none. The next day, the covers were full, but only the covers which were along a stream which flowed from west to east toward Michigan's Lake Huron. The birds planned to use the lakeshore and its marshy pockets for food, and let the westerly winds of the previous night push them along that stream toward the lake. From there, it is a simple matter of heading south, waiting for the north winds of autumn to blow them that way.

The birds, then, use the streams as a source of food and navigation, and the stars to help in navigation. Pick out a river system that fits the description and as shown on the accompanying map. Wait for clear skies, note the wind direction during the nighttime hours, and hunt the proper river valley—it works!

Another way of keeping tabs on the migration is to note the age and sex of the birds you shoot. Females and, to a certain extent, the immature birds (those hatched the previous spring) migrate earlier. The males, especially the adults, migrate later when the weather may be downright miserable. This is probably a way of insuring that the breeding females are kept safer, and the young are kept intact for the next season's reproduction.

The males, on the other hand, may hang around up north

longer, perhaps to better imprint breeding grounds. Maybe they are capable of migrating under less favorable conditions because their smaller body size enables them to fight the headwinds a bit better than the chunky females and juveniles.

At any rate, if a shooter finds that he is taking mostly females, he can look for longer action throughout the season. If, however, he is shooting only males when the season opens, he can pretty well figure that the main populations of females and immatures have passed him by before the season ever opened.

Overall dry or wet years also influence the migration. The fall of 1976 was a dry one in Michigan. Covers were parched by drought, fires were a problem, and the woodcock were gone before mid-October in my covers. Next year, 1977, late summer and early autumn rains dampened the covers and the birds hung around into November. What this means, naturally, is that dry years drive the worms deep into the ground. Once the food supply is reduced the birds leave with the first favorable winds. If the hunter plans his hunting days with a time schedule in mind, then a dry year means that he should concentrate his hunting right near the season's opener. Likewise, in dry years, streams with the biggest water flow and more damp cover will hold the most birds. In dry years hunt the bigger streams, and hunt them early in the season.

Dry conditions also mean that hunting should be concentrated early in the day, when the birds are feeding to take advantage of the available moisture from dew. Feeding covers, then, are the place to look at first light, because the birds may still be in them during the dry years.

As migration progresses, time becomes critical for the woodcock. If the favorable winds have not been present, the birds continue to wait for them. All the time, the days grow shorter, the nights colder, and the food supply is reduced.

When this happens, the birds—now only the males are staged and ready to go—will take advantage of windless nights to migrate. This flighting of birds on calm evenings is the result of not wanting to get caught with their feathers down.

They prefer a tailwind, but will go when there is no wind if that's the best they can get.

At this time, any large, favorable wind will completely scour clean the covers in a particular watershed, resulting in the huge "flights." Usually, a north wind does this best. Over the preceding weeks, the birds have used the various east and west winds to move along feeder creeks or streams to the main north/south land formation-riverbed, moraine, valley, or lakeshore. They are thus ganged up, awaiting the final push south. When the north wind comes, all the migrants leave at once, thus prompting shooters to the south to proclaim that woodcock will flight on the wings of an autumn "norther." In effect, they could have had great shooting all fall had they hunted the east and west streambeds when the winds were from that direction. As it is, they only got shooting at the birds just as they were leaving the locale, maybe even the state, because they only considered the effect of that one type of wind. They overlooked all those winds that preceded the north wind and put the birds into the north/south valley to begin with.

Now that this has been digested, how can the shooter take advantage of it to find his covers?

Topographical maps tell the location of rivers, streams, and even mark out such areas as bogs, or marshland. Acid bogs should be avoided because they hold few worms, and thus few woodcock. However, backwater low spots along streams are dandy places to find woodcock, and the maps also give the location of such features as buildings, which may tell you where to ask permission.

Naturally, this brings us to a discussion of covers. Woodcock have, essentially, two types of cover: feeding, and resting covers. I prefer to think of the resting covers as waiting covers, where the birds spend their daylight hours waiting for darkness to feed, and waiting for the winds to come up, which will move them along their chosen migration route.

In any event, feeding covers are often hunted when there are no, or few birds in them. Feeding covers are essentially a nighttime proposition. True, birds will be found there almost any time of day, but the really productive covers are the waiting spots.

I've found woodcock in cornfields, on front lawns, on sandy ridges covered with sumac, and in tangles that a rabbit couldn't penetrate. However, most of these are exceptions. Essentially, a woodcock wants cover that he can while away the daylight hours in relative comfort, moving about, dusting, or just resting up for the migration. Birds that are migrating are not going to waste precious calories by flying five miles from a feeding cover to a waiting cover; the two will be nearby one another.

With food being the primary influence here, it is best to first locate the feeding covers along your chosen stream.

Alders are a dead giveaway, providing that they are under 12 feet in height. Any larger, and they start to die. This causes the soil to change its chemical makeup, and the worms leave. No food, no woodcock.

Find alders mixed with some second growth aspen (poplar), none or a few knee-high marsh grasses that permit movement underneath, put it all near a stream, make the bottom rich and black and moist, and mister, you'll find woodcock. If the cover is 5 to 10 years old, so much the better.

Check to see if a cow pasture is nearby within 200 yards. Cows can "fertilize" the open ground at a fantastic rate, as any farm boy knows, and the worms—and thus woodcock—are there during the dark hours. A patch of alders that the local farmer has been pasturing is a good spot, too. Alders mean damp, fertile soil, and thus woodcock. Alders can fix nitrogen directly into the soil and this is perfect for worms and grubs— 85% of the bird's diet. If this combination is along a streambed, you're in business.

Even ditches cut across open pasture land will hold a few birds, especially in wet years. The key is moisture for feeding cover.

Your average hunter, however, is going to enjoy most of his sport in the waiting covers. These, as mentioned earlier, are located close to the feeding covers, and the best ones almost universally follow a certain criteria: second growth aspen, birch and a few alders all under 20 feet tall and within arm's reach of one another. These are mixed with a knee-high canopy of bracken ferns. The ferns provide the shelter from the sun, rain and airborne predators, and the trees serve about the same purpose. When the trees age, natural attrition thins them out and thus cuts down on the amount of protection they offer. That's why a woodcock cover will outgrow its usefulness after the trees are over 25 feet in height—no shelter.

The ground cover should not be thick. Annual grasses that grow very close together don't allow the birds to move around during the day, and so they won't be there. The ferns offer a sheltering canopy above the bird's head, but allow him to walk around and discuss the stock market with his buddies.

One area that shooters can find good action in is the sumac and fern-covered hillsides adjacent to feeding cover. The sumac bushes grow up to 12 feet in height and serve the same purpose as the aspen trees. Remember, the waiting cover need not be good feeding cover, but should provide shelter from the elements, such as rain and hot sun, protection from predators, and should be close to feeding cover.

Remember, however, that even though everything may look fine, if the cover you've located is not near one of the streams that the woodcock use for migrational aids, you'll find few birds. You must hunt their flyways, described earlier, to be successful.

Hunting good waiting cover can also lead the shooter to some good action with the woodcock's sometimes cover-mate, the ruffed grouse.

Most woodcock are taken by grouse hunters who shoot the smaller birds incidentally. With proper planning, the gunner can have woodcock covers, grouse covers, and combination covers.

Most such combination covers are really marginal for either species, but seem to follow a certain pattern. When looking for combination covers, a shooter should note some special patterns.

Deserted farmsteads, yielding to pioneer forest plants are great combination covers. With nearby streams, they are also hotspots for woodcock as the primary quarry.

One of the things to look for is low, second growth aspen, birch, or red maple. This pioneer forest type is prevalent throughout the northern tier of states, and is suitable habitat for ruffed grouse and as waiting cover for woodcock.

The key is to find this cover in proximity to streams, or close by what can be called woodcock feeding cover. The 'cock will fly to the waiting cover after feeding; the grouse will never leave it.

The hunter, then, should be alert for any of the myriad of grouse food sources, patches of heavy cover, a few coniferous trees, and if this is located near a stream which woodcock are using, a combination cover is a distinct possibility.

One of the best ways is to note the slopes of a stream valley. As the elevation rises, typically, the vegetation will change from plants which are native to wet soils, to those which are native to drier soils, such as aspen/birch/maple association. Where this vegetation change takes place is where the combination cover will be located. Such elevations offer grouse a variety of food and cover within walking distance.

In dry years, grouse will be concentrated near water because that will be where the available food is located, and combination covers are easiest to find in such years. Rainfall scatters both grouse and woodcock throughout their range.

Hunting a combination cover can be a real challenge, because when the dog points, it is hard to get set for the shot. Grouse tend to fly toward thicker cover, while woodcock like to fly toward holes in the canopy. About the time a shooter is set for a woodcock flush, a grouse bores out low and over his head, making for the thick cover behind the startled gunner. At times like this, one's vocabulary of choice words seems limited and repetitive.

Whenever somebody does a field study, the more intellectual types want to talk about data, methods and materials, and bases for drawing conclusions. Being basically a lowbrow, let me try to explain.

Essentially, I started the study in the fall of 1973, and continued it through the fall of 1978. For the first five seasons, I observed, recorded and analyzed to come up with this hypothesis. The last year and since then, I took my own advice and tried it. It works.

To do such a study of wild creatures, one must factor out as many variables as possible. My study was done in the lower Peninsula of Michigan—which is as close as you'll get to a hint about where my covers are! I hunted only on private land, closed to all but me, to take out the factor of hunter disturbance, and within 15 miles of the nearest class A recording weather station.

Each time out, I hunted the same covers as the previous time, usually on weekends, and compared my Saturday and Sunday results.

Just in case I was a little sloppy in my sampling—with a good dog and gun—I calculated that a flight had taken place if there were either twice as many birds there as the day before, or none when there were some yesterday.

This way, I knew when a "trickle through" migration had occurred. Then, I correlated the results with every known weather factor I could get the U.S. Climatological Survey to cough up: wind speed, wind direction, temperature, visibility, cloud cover, rainfall or snowfall, chill factor (I had to figure this myself) and so on.

Finally it all came together when I made plastic transparencies of covers I hunted, laid them over a topographical map of the three river systems I hunted, and started to extrapolate.

Seems the only factor constant was cloud cover and wind direction. But, strangely, the wind direction had to be as I described earlier, from a direction the woodcock were going to use as a migrational aid anyway. Clear skies meant, I guessed, better celestial navigation, and the wind meant they had a tail breeze along the chosen route of migration to an area from which they could push south.

Now, I have a hunch that this would work just as nicely in the valleys and passes in the Appalachian Mountains in

New England. Picture this: There are several mountains, each with their separating valleys and the vegetation and damp ground native to those valleys. Valleys mean weathered rock—soil—and the damp soil spells worms, the woodcock's diet.

Is this little bird going to leave this gravy train to try to fly over a mountain just because the wind is from the north or it gets a little nippy? Hardly.

Instead, he awaits a breeze that will push him down his home valley, let's say it's an east/west valley. Now, that favorable wind has come up, and he moves 15 miles down the valley until he comes to another valley, streambed, or range of mountains heading north/south. He holes up, stokes up his burners on fat nightcrawlers and grubs, and waits out the sun.

The next night, the wind shifts and blows from the south. Still he waits, because the wind would be right in his face if he tried to migrate. The next night the wind is still wrong, and the next night, there is no wind.

Now, he makes a choice. He has no tailwind, but yesterday's more slanted rays from the sun told him, "Be gone from here," so he takes off, without a tailwind, but at least with no headwind.

He flies through the night, heading ever southward. Without warning, the south winds pick up again, and he lands to lay over and wait it out, feeding voraciously.

Still, the winds blow from the south. They are warm, but his imprinting tells him he must go. Finally, the wind dies and is barely blowing from the south. He goes tonight, fighting a slight head-on breeze, thinking only of his pumping wings and his wintering grounds in the south.

He lays over another day. Maybe in the Caanan Valley of West Virginia. This night, the wind blows strong from the north. He leaves with his face still muddy from foraging, fighting to keep the wind at his back. The skies are clear, perfect for navigation. He is tired when he lands as the fiery orb rises, but he has made many miles and expended relatively few calories in the process. His valley is nearby as his food supply. He has jogged back and forth a bit with the valley, sometimes switching back to fly a bit north with the lay of the land, or in a great sweeping arc as the valley oxbows. But what of it? The food supply was close, his stars told him where he was, and now the wintering grounds are but a few miles away.

He was not alone this last night. Other woodcock, backed up by the days and nights of south wind, came down as well, and a real live "flight" hits the covers of northern Carolina that morning. Had the winds been favorable all along during the migration, he would have seen just a few others, because each bird migrates with his own unique biological clock. The locals would have spoken of mere trickles of migrants, and cursed the deadly shooting of the Yankee gunners, not knowing the numbers were constant, it was the rate that varied.

He would spend a leisurely winter in the Southland, probing for worms, moving from cover to cover as whim and fancy drove him. In the spring, the lengthening days would cause glands in his body to change, to secrete hormones which in turn caused the sex glands in both males and females to enlarge and demand use. When the rays were exactly right, he and others of his kind would head north again, dancing along the way, and finally ending up in the home covers of the home valley again.

Eggs would be laid, chicks watched over, and by the midsummer, the young birds would rival the adults in size, if not yet vitality. The summer would be spent in these covers, and in the decreasing daylight hours of autumn, the ritual would begin again. The hens and young would go first, as nature protects the young crop and the proven breeders. The males would stay until conditions were less favorable, the better to imprint the home breeding grounds maybe.

At any rate, by the end of September, in the New England and Great Lakes states, the birds would be readying themselves for the migratory quest. Not as the magnificent flocks of geese would they go, and unlike Capistrano's swallows, no migration by which to check the calendar. They would go when they were ready, each as an individual.

Before migration occurs, and indeed while the summer

sun still burns high and warm, the birds start a "shuffling" process of moving from cover to cover. This breaks up the family groups, and is not uncommon in nature. In fact, it is probably a method of preventing inbreeding among nestlings when they return to breed the next spring.

In late August, in the northern climes, the woodcock will be shuffling about, moving from cover to cover, until the migrational urge strikes them. It is at this time that they will head south. Many shooters, afield in the late summer, have claimed to witness migration. Not true, they've just seen the late summer shuffle.

The migration ritual has been repeated for the last 9,000 years, since the last glacial age ended, giving the birds something to migrate north to.

And between the birds and their wintering grounds each autumn stand scores of men with 20-gauge shotguns ready to pluck the excess from this bounty. Not as killers, but as more or less inefficient harvesters, themselves acting as an evolutionary agent, taking the slow, the weak, the stupid. The best survive to whistle their wings in countless generations of autumns.

There is, indeed, need for far more study of this bird. I've given you the results of some rather exhaustive studies I've done on autumn migrations. I've used every tool I could, short of tying on some electric homing devices, yet this is not enough.

That what I've described to you works, have no doubt. Locate some covers, try out this system and enjoy some shooting. I don't think knowing when or where the birds will be next detracts from the mystery and allure of the hunt at all. Knowing that the gales are going to drive down the mallards from the north subtracts not a bit from the anticipation and glitter that the duck hunter nurtures. Knowing that the old buck will emerge from the woods just at twilight doesn't dull the senses of the deer hunter, and knowing that the Churchyard Covey will be right there in that little corner pocket along about six P.M. doesn't tarnish the hunt for the southern quail shooter.

Instead, I've found that it has heightened the thrill of woodcock hunting for me. I can say I know the birds a bit better, a bit more intimately, than I did before, and I'm grateful for the chance.

But, the bird needs more study. We need to know the effects of pesticides, and herbicides, and even sunspots, sonic booms and things that go bump in the night. Because we can only hope to help the "little russet feller" if we know some of his secrets, some of his long hidden complexities. We need funds, maybe those provided by the establishment of a non-waterfowl migratory bird stamp or something like it. With these funds, we can pay the men who make the studies, that help the birds that give us such pleasure.

Time will tell about the woodcock, but right now, his stock is high and rising—America is bullish on woodcock. Let's keep it that way.

Several times, so far, I've referred to wet and dry years as they influence the movement of grouse and woodcock.

With woodcock, being migratory and thus more mobile, the effects are often quite pronounced and have definite impacts on the fall gunning, especially as far as gunning native birds is concerned.

For starters, most shooters find most of their woodcock sport on native birds. Time and the red gods being what they are, it is possible to miss the flights, and therefore the sport for the whole season.

If a gunner misses a chance to hunt the natives, however, a season can be a bust. True, the native birds shouldn't be pounded too heavily, but they can and do provide the lion's share of shooting without visibly damaging the population.

Since woodcock are precocial in their nesting and growth, the chicks are ready to fly and almost indistinguishable from adults in a matter of weeks. Their need for food, as discussed earlier, is almost staggering. Because of this, any drastic drop in the food supply over a broad area of their range is almost catastrophic to the birds.

Let's take a look first at the wet years, the years when the rains never seem to quit all the way through the summer, and

when you can't keep up with the grass and the flower beds—
not that you would want to.

A wet year, as far as the fall woodcock season goes, is
really a great time for shooters. As noted awhile back, the
birds are given to flying south more leisurely, and food is in
abundant supply. Soil moisture holds the worms the birds eat
close to the surface, and the woodcock are rarely pressed for a
beakful of wriggling protein.

With this in mind, the smart gunner will search in the
areas that the birds will be using for resting cover. With no
need to worry and hurry about food, the birds follow a fairly
predictable daily pattern. They fly to food at dusk, mill around
in the cover until dawn, and then fly to resting cover, usually
second growth aspen or similar cover that provides the necessary overhead shelter from airborne predators.

For the shooter, this predictability also means that the
birds will be in the areas they were scouted in during the
spring and summer. There has been little or no movement
during the summer because there's been no need to move.
Food, shelter and cover are all present, so they while away the
summer and fall, waiting the winds of autumn to move them
southward. The man who bands woodcock in the spring will
find many of his banded birds not too far away during the fall
gunning season—kind of like a reunion, but with different in-
tentions.

But, the wet year is often a rarity. The dry year means another whole batch of rules.

The summer of 1979 had been quite dry in the Great
Lakes region where I live. My partner, Mark Sutton, and I had
little success locating woodcock in their usual haunts. We
were stumped.

Finally, we got out some topographical maps and started
looking for some alternate covers, with soil moisture the key
criterion.

We located a swamp with some birds, but nothing like we
expected. Finally, out of frustration more than anything else,
we headed for high country—the top of a 1,000 foot high gla-

cial moraine that bisects part of Michigan's Lower Peninsula. There we found birds.

But, we found them in tiny pockets—a bird here, another there, in small depressions that held some residual moisture. Some of the pockets were less than 20 feet in diameter and held native willows or a few alders. It was good shooting, but hard to figure out.

We deduced that the birds had moved from their usual summering grounds shortly after the chicks could fly. They had taken refuge from the dry conditions atop the moraine perhaps to take advantage of the lingering moisture found because of the higher elevation's heavier fog or dew, about the only moisture likely to be present that summer.

To see if we were right, we headed for the high country early one Saturday morning near the end of September. Standing on a promontory that offered good visibility, we were able to locate the moist pockets by the fog that radiated upward. No birds traded in or out of these fog pockets, so we weren't too optimistic. But, after the sun was well up, we proceeded to work the pockets, one at a time, and the shooting was rewarding.

Again, there were no areas that held huge numbers of feathered targets, but each pocket held a bird or two. We limited out before noon.

Apparently, and I'd like to repeat "apparently," the birds had shifted to the high country and had taken up residence for the summer. The high ground gave them what they needed, and they had dispersed themselves so well that no single bird was overcrowded by his colleagues. Thus, the food supply lasted through the drought. They also apparently stayed put once within such a pocket until migration.

As far as the flights are concerned, dry-year woodcock will very rarely dally along the way. They sense that food is in short supply and go on the first available tailwind. This can make for great shooting if you're there when they go through. If you're not, that's the breaks.

Tom Prawdzik, a grouse and woodcock expert with the

Michigan Department of Natural Resources, notes that this phenomenon is not uncommon.

"We've got reports of birds moving east from Wisconsin to Michigan, up north within the state, and south, all before the flights start. They really reshuffle before migration."

This reshuffling very well could be a result of the lack of moisture. The food supply is depleted quickly and the birds must go elsewhere. High ground just may be the place. This high ground could be a mountain terrace, a moraine, or in another part of the state where the moisture content is greater, and therefore the food supply increased.

During the shooting season itself, attention must be paid to the rainfall conditions between hunts. A slaking rain during the week can move the birds away from an area where you found them last weekend, and to another area.

Conversely, a dry spell can move them to the high ground or several miles away to an area that a sudden shower saturated. These hit-and-miss rainstorms will move the birds around quickly, and the hunter has to stay mobile.

During the '79 season, Sutton and I found some woodcock near a creek with a good growth of alders. We shot some right down in the thick stuff and had great sport, though we didn't hurt the population much because mostly we missed.

The next week, that area had a sudden shower that lasted several hours while the nearby areas weren't dampened. Returning to that same cover, we found nary a bird in the wet places, but instead they were on a sunny, second-growth hillside near the feeding area. The rain had dampened the ground enough that food was available elsewhere, and they were loafing with full tummies. During dry times, then, the birds are reluctant to leave the food-bearing covers, but when the rains come they spend the daylight hours in the traditional resting covers, awaiting nightfall.

The lesson? The woodcock is a mobile bird. If you want to bag him, you'll have to be mobile too.

Steve Smith

Voices From Woodcock Country

Although I didn't know it at the time, the first good
woodcock dog I ever saw was an orange Belton setter
about the size of a young heifer. His owner was one of
those florid-faced men who looked as though he had slept in
the bow tie he was wearing. He had the build of a butcher and
the soft, low voice of a choir master. He spoke to his dog in
tones that carried affection, trust, and complete understanding. This was the sort of companionship that you knew had
many years of close living and working together behind it. I
could barely imagine the man driving or walking anywhere
without the big setter at his side.

They had devised a curious and thoroughly effective
method of hunting the bottom covers. The cap-and-bow-tie
would find a spot to his liking and stand still. The dog would
then amble out about 40 or 50 yards and begin a slow series of
circles that either ended up in a point (not really a point, but
more of a standing-still and looking-at where the bird sat) or
back with his owner. The hunter would then walk on to another likely spot, and the dog would begin his circling back all
over again.

He noticed my watching him one afternoon, and when he
called me over, I broke open my single-shot 20-gauge, adjusted the couple of rabbits I had in my sack, and joined him.
"That's Jack," he said, nodding toward the setter, who looked
away as if ashamed to be seen so close to a cottontail brush-

jumper. "You can hunt with me if you'd like to try a few woodcock, and if Jack pushes out a rabbit, why, just go ahead and shoot it. He won't pay any attention."

We walked awhile together, silent, until he found a spot to his liking. "Stand over there," he said, pointing to a scrub birch clump. "If a bird gets up, or Jack goes on point, you get first shot, okay?"

I nodded, and Jack began his curious corkscrewing through the woods, looking over at me now and then, as if to confirm his opinion that he was working for what was obviously the world's worst wingshot. Jack had me pegged about right. The full-choked single 20 was a lightning strike on a sitting rabbit, but I'd wasted enough heavy 6's on various birds to know that I was not born to shake the throne of Fred Kimble. I dreaded both the flushed bird and the pointed one, and missed a chance at each. I told the man that I'd rather watch, and, in the next hour, I saw him take four birds with four right barrels of his side-by-side L. C. Smith.

When we came out of the brook bottom, his car was there by the edge of the road. I thanked him and told him I hoped we'd meet again, but declined his offer of a ride, on the chance of picking up another rabbit or two on the walk home. "Is your mother a good cook?" he asked. She wasn't, but I didn't know that then, so I said yes. He reached around inside his hunting coat and after smoothing each one, dropped the four birds in my rabbit sack. I started to protest, but he stopped me short by saying, "Jack and I get our share. Just remember where you see some when you're hunting, and next time we meet you can take *me* along."

Country people, back then, didn't pry each other with a lot of questions, so I never learned his name, nor he mine. I assume now, looking back, that we had hit the last part of the flight, and we never again met in the woods, nor did I ever see his roadster parked along any of the roads I walked. But we did hunt together, in my imagination, many a time after. Sitting in the oak and hickory watching for squirrels, I could see myself with a bird dog of my own and an identical L. C. Smith, leading the old hunter to a secret alder cover teeming with woodcock. There I would distinguish myself by never having to dirty the left barrel. A lot of time has gone by, but it hasn't diminished this dream one whit—and neither has any of it come true.

The half-mystery of my first meeting with a woodcock hunter, and the even greater mystery of the bird itself, lit a fire that has consumed me ever since. It has also consumed countless days of meandering bottom covers peppered with birches or silvered with popple. It has consumed countless days of fooling with a variety of shotguns in the endless (I'm sure) search for the precisely right combination of weight, balance, barrel length, and choke. And it has consumed countless days of fooling with various bird dogs in another endless search for the precise amounts of bidability, range, nose, and companionship. I count those times among my most treasured hours.

The best woodcock covers are often not the kind you'll see in a painting. Nor are they to be analyzed by soil type, cover, sun, or shade. I have found woodcock in such unlikely places as the midst of ideal quail cover in northeast Texas; in high, rock-strewn ledges where the scrawny evergreens send out root tendrils in the moss searching for soil; and even along the edge of my driveway. The true woodcock gunner finds himself drawn to what suits his nature—not necessarily the ideal.

My instincts lead me to where I can hear the swamp-edge soil sucking lightly at my leather-topped rubber boots. I enjoy the possibility of discovering a hidden spring, a trickle of brook packed with watercress and, of course, the telltale little splashes of whitewash that indicate visitors. I like being down out of the wind with the pungent smells of mayapples, skunk cabbage, and hemlock. I like the feeling of constant change you get in the low country—as against the semi-permanence of wind-ridden high ridges that seem unalterable.

My setters like the low country, too. Once long ago, a lovely, orange-ticked white ghost named Jag, delighted in flinging herself in the cool mud and coming out looking like a troll. If there aren't any woodcock, there are almost always frogs, snakes, or the occasional muskrat to worry up. There is always something.

There are those gunners who say that the actual shooting of a woodcock is anticlimactic, claiming that the birds offer no challenge to the expert shot. In reply, I use a common synonym for a byproduct of cattle raising. I would like to take some of these so-called experts to one of my favorite bottom covers. I defy them to take a limit of four birds with sixteen shells. I further defy them to throw their hats on the ground and have them hit, for the place I would take them is what you might call a thicket—if the word thicket still carries the strength I attribute to it. Here you will hear woodcock in numbers; you will see several; but you'll be able to swing on very few. And I love it. This is hunting; this is getting down to what it's all about. This is coming home proud that you took a couple of birds from a pocket-dark, shadow-ridden, fight-your-way-through alder cover. This is 24-inch-barrel, no-choke, shoot-from-the hip cover. This is where your soft-footed setter sounds like a moose as she climbs over and through stuff that you can't. This is where you discover that woodcock don't hold like all the books tell you, where birds fly like silent puffs of smoke. This is where it really is!

There are famous woodcock covers where you can go out and take a limit between a late breakfast and lunch. But I don't like them. These are usually not feeding covers, but the resting ones that birds use after a long and arduous flight. You're pushing out birds that are tired, if not exhausted. This is not hunting, and I want no part of it. Neither do your fine Michigan sportsmen, or your classic New England gunners, or those lucky enough to spend October in New Brunswick. They love this bird above all and believe in a fair chase. They know the times and places where they can feel proud to take a bird or two for a companion piece to a sturdy red wine. They want to earn it the hard way, because woodcock deserve no less.

The oldtime woodcock hunters that I knew liked most to hunt alone. They carted tall, long-headed Gordon or English setters with a slow, thorough pace. There was no hint of hurry, no mention of covering so many miles, no bragging about bags. They'd come back and sit in the country store and tell you as much about what was going on in the woods as they would about the hunt itself—often more. They were quiet men whom, I believe, found a reward in an afternoon with a dog and their old 20-bore Parkers that was more personal and fulfilling than many of us, time-ridden and pushed by inner demands, can ever feel today. They mussed with puppies, and felt more comfortable around horses than they did with cars. They talked about old orchards that still bore Pound Sweets; about bee trees, seeing trout, and where Indian moccasin grew. They remembered the name of everyone else's dogs and chatted about them with enthusiasm and honest affection.

In fact, they would talk at length about almost any-thing—except exactly where they had been gunning. You'd ask Marvin or Ely where they thought some birds might be and one would say, "Well, you might find a couple up around back of Culver's Lake," thereby loosely directing you to an area of about 15 square miles. Only a kid would have had the naiveté to even ask. The other oldtimers wouldn't have wasted their hard-cider breath, knowing the answer would bear only the haziest relation to the facts of the matter. Even back then there were the jokes about taking you out sometime "only I'd have to blindfold both you and Old Jack."

I'd see these local legends now and then at the store. They'd buy a box of shells for sixty cents, or, if times were hard, a half a dozen or so single shells for three cents apiece. A box of crackers and a good wedge of rat cheese was a dime. For the dog there'd be some home-made cornbread in the car. If it was cider-making time, 15 cents would fill a gallon jug (no charge for the cooling damp feed sack to wrap it in). To me, more or less gun-less and dog-less, they were giants with skills and knowledge beyond my personal hope. How could I ever be like them? Nothing in my foreseeable future promised an English or a Gordon. The Bakers and LeFevers, the Reming-tons and Parkers, the Smiths and Foxes that could be seen, from a distance, at the hardware store—they were as remote to me as ever getting my chores done. The leggings and the high-laced leather boots were the uniforms of generals seen through the eyes of a career private.

Yet, I knew that someday my turn would come. What I did not suspect was that it would be in another, less glamorous, time. I felt a great loss, driving back through this country with my English setter and my 16-gauge L. C. Smith, knowing that the companions I so desperately wanted to talk with were no longer around. Nor was the store with its 10-cent cheese and crackers, its 60-cent shells, and cider mill, with its tin cup and full bucket for the visitor to sample while he waited for a fresh pressing. The twisting dirt roads that had held such adventure and promise were either oiled or paved. All that was left were some of the woodcock covers, and those I mostly had to myself. Yes, I took my pleasures in them—but how I longed for a country store that welcomed your dog, or for an oldtimer to swing and admire my L. C. Smith the way I had so often seen them do with each other's guns. How I wished for the questions about where it was that Little Ben and I had done so well—and to have been able to rock back in my chair, fuss with my pipe, and describe an area that was close, but not too close, while a farmboy scratched Ben's ears and looked at me with wonder and envy.

What I wouldn't give to have heard as I left the store that priceless sentence that I had so often heard about Marvin or Ely: *"That Hilly there, him and that Ben dog is about as good a pair as you'll find anywhere when it comes to woodcock."*

I do hear it now and then, but like so much of what we yearn for, it is only a man hearing voices in his imagination from a time that he lives in all alone.

Gene Hill

Ruffed Grouse—
The Upland King

To many people who buy hunting licenses each year, the reason for such purchases weighs about 1½ pounds, is kind of a brown color, and flies like some type of jet fighter. He is the ruffed grouse, glamour boy and king of the upland shooting hill. He is hard to find, harder to bring to hand, and is unsurpassed on the table. He counts captains of industry, heads of governmental units, and 11-year-old farm boys among his admirers, and treats all equally—with disdain.

He is the crowned head of birddom, if that's a word, and the reason literally millions of shotguns have been sold. His numbers have been shot almost to extinction in parts, but he keeps coming back.

He has grown smarter and wiser, and perhaps faster and more elusive as the years have progressed, and he is above all wild. The wilderness can never be bred out of the grouse and have him submit to pen rearing. If this is attempted, he becomes nothing but a docile chicken, and the allure is gone.

No, he must be kept in the wild state, and his numbers, thanks to proper management and informed and enlightened managers, are increasing.

Old *Bonasa umbellus* is the mystical thunderbird of legend, he is the bird that Midwesterners think of when New England shooting is the topic, and the bird that New Englanders travel to the Midwest and Great Lakes states to find in better numbers. He is The King.

W. J. Schaldach

His enemies are legion. He or his eggs are eaten by various species of foxes, hawks, owls, weasels, housecats, bobcats, skunks and raccoons.

His habitat is replaced by blacktop jungles and housing developments, yet he survives.

And even those who seek him are a bit on the stuffy side, some say. Grouse hunters are given to talking in terms of "forward allowance" rather than "lead." They prefer clothing other than filling station coveralls when hunting, and usually choose a small-bore double-gun with which to do their shooting—meager though it may be.

The grouse hunter of today is not the expert woodsman, usually, that his market-gunning ancestor was, yet neither is he the cold-blooded harvester-like gent from the past. While the old market gunner took grouse with the same feeling you and I would get from pulling radishes from the garden, he was none-the-less effective. His efficiency has given us the super-smart, super-wild grouse of today, for he culled the dumbbells year after year, generation after generation.

Much has been written about the market gunners of the last century, and their deliberate, deadly shotgunning. However, my conversations with a few of the oldtimers led me to believe that many more birds were picked from the trees of winter with a small caliber rifle than were ever killed with a market gunner's smoothbore. Many more were snared with wire loops, and the numbers sold on the open market must have been astounding.

Today's gunner feels that the sport is in the seeking, not the killing. Although it may sound snobbish, let me quote a friend of mine and fellow grouse and woodcock enthusiast.

"There are those that will fish for carp with doughballs, and those that take brook trout on dryflies. There are those who like a well-chilled chablis, and those who take their beer from a can. There are those who prefer a speedboat pulling a water skier, and those who enjoy being pushed about by a stiff wind in the mainsail. Lastly, there is everybody else and those who gun grouse."

Steve Smith

Grouse Habits
and Habitat

The ruffed grouse of the present age is no longer the "fool hen" of yesteryear, and in well hunted areas, is probably the smartest creature to inhabit the woodlands—and that includes the hunter seeking him. At times, the grouse seem difficult to bag, or even see. At other times, they seem to have left entirely, so few are their numbers.

Before we take a look at where to find him, let's examine the habits the grouse has developed over the centuries to see if there are any facts that can be gleaned to better aid the hunter.

The ruffed grouse's year begins in the spring, when the snow of the north country begins to melt and the days lengthen. This lengthening process stirs the mating urge in friend grouse, and the courtship procedure begins. The male will find a handy log or stump, and strut his stuff by beating the air frantically against his breast, creating a booming, or "drumming" sound which can be heard for nearly a half mile when conditions are right.

The female, hearing this sound, coyly trots over to investigate, and the strutting male finally induces her to mate. During this time, the female becomes more dominant, and the lovesick cockbird will follow her everywhere. After mating, the pair splits up, and the male will go back to his drumming, seeking more conquests.

In about three weeks the female will look for a nice section of hardwood trees and build a ground nest near the base of a tree, fallen log, or some other handy prominence for better protection. The 10 or 11, average, eggs are laid, and after all are in the nest, she broods them. The young birds are hatched in 23 or 24 days.

Unlike the woodcock, the ruffed grouse suffers from high nest and chick mortality. Egg-stealing crows, weasels, red squirrels, some species of snakes, skunks and raccoons all conspire to keep grouse fledgling numbers low. On top of that, a certain number of eggs are infertile anyway, and the female senses which ones, rolling them from the nest.

Once hatched, the young birds follow Momma everywhere, and feed primarily on insects for the first 10 days to two weeks of their lives. Insects are high in protein, the builder of muscle, and the young grouse will feed voraciously on bugs until they are about two weeks old, when the first short flights are attempted. Young broods of grouse inhabit new aspen growth of less than 8 years of age because of high insect population.

During this early period, the grouse's worst enemy is cold rain. Mother Grouse cannot protect all the young, and the cold rain kills the young quite effectively. Because of all the perils of chickhood, a survival rate of four chicks from a nest of 9 to 14 eggs is considered good.

The young birds start flying in earnest after about a month, and by six-weeks-old they are colored up like the parents.

Shortly after flight becomes part of the young grouse's repertoire, the birds begin to break up the family groups. This is usually accomplished by the end of September at latest, and is nature's way of preventing inbreeding, which can ruin a strain of grouse. At this time, the grouse may move miles from the original homesite, or less than 500 yards if habitat is right and underpopulated. At such times, grouse have been known to fly into telephone lines, windows on houses, walk stupidly in front of automobiles, and otherwise seem bent on self destruction. In the end, the original family of grouse is well scattered, and fattening in the fall uplands.

At this time, the grouse are more likely to be found in the second growth aspen that is 8 to 15 years of age, feeding on the many foods available in that highly productive forest type.

Trying to find grouse based upon the contents of an opened crop is chancey at best. The grouse is not finickey in his tastes, and eats nearly 1,000 different types of food throughout his range. Everything from acorns the size of his head to poison ivy berries are fair fare for the grouse, and green leaves are always a delicacy.

As winter approaches, and food supply is limited, the grouse of late autumn feeds in the older stands of aspen— from 15 to 25 years of age and as big around as your leg. Here, he spends much time "budding," or eating the buds from the male aspen tree. If this area contains a small stand of conifers to better cut the wind, so much the better. His feet have grown feathery snowshoes, and he walks where he wants to go atop the fluffy snow. While he will continue to roost in trees, he now prefers the conifers to save previous calories as the snow piles deep underfoot.

On extremely cold nights, the grouse will burrow or fly into a handy snowbank and make himself a makeshift igloo of the insulating snow. Inside this downy blanket, temperatures may be 50 degrees warmer than the outside temperatures, and as morning approaches, he pokes his head out and goes his fanciful way.

Once, while seeking wintertime bunnies, I stepped into the middle of a small clearing and stopped to light my pipe. As I did, no less than seven grouse burst skyward. I lost my pipe from my gaping mouth.

Because of such experiences, many shooters figure that the grouse flock up in the winter, like chickadees. In fact, the birds are just herded together by the lack of available cover due to winter's onslaught. Where in the fall they are scattered and far between, winter causes all birds in a given locale to seek the best cover available. At such times, a large number of grouse flushes in a short period of time is not uncommon. In addition, they will flush nearly underfoot, probably wanting to conserve strength as much as possible and hoping the intruder will pass them by.

During this time of year, mortality is high. The fox, the owl, and various hawks will take grouse because their food supply is also limited. Cold saps the strength of weaker birds, and the rare ice storm can turn the grouse's comfortable snow burrow into an ice encrusted tomb, where he starves to death. Ice also can close the nostrils of a grouse, causing slow suffocation, because this part of the anatomy contains no warming blood vessels to melt the ice. Only about 30 percent of the birds alive at hatching time are alive to breed the next spring. Hunting pressure has no real effect. Shooting seems to take the excess which would have died of other causes anyway. In fact, hunting can actually help a population stay healthy.

Grouse are somewhat finicky when it comes to breeding, and, like tenement residents, do not react well to crowded conditions. When an area becomes populated to maximum—about one breeding pair per 10 acres of ground—the grouse may stop breeding. Hunting, by trimming some birds back, keeps the population more or less on the upswing all the time so this saturation point is never reached.

This may be the reason behind the seven-year cycle of grouse populations. As populations rise, the stabilizing factor is reproduction. When populations are low, the grouse breed like mad. When populations reach saturation, they taper off and the lows occur. This is only conjecture, and there are many unanswered questions, such as why the highs and lows seem to move from west to east across the northern tier of states. I know a good year in Wisconsin, for example, will be duplicated the next year in my home state of Michigan.

During the fall gunning season, the shooter has to pay attention to the conditions of the summer to help locate grouse. A dry year tends to concentrate the birds near water. Grouse seem to get all the moisture they need from the food they take in, so this movement toward water is probably to take advantage of the lusher vegetation growth that covers streamcourses. This jungle of plant life, compared to the drought-plagued open woodlands in a dry year, offers the grouse more food and better cover.

Inversely, during wet years, the birds are more scattered and flushes, though fewer in a day, are more regular and spaced, giving your jangled nerves a chance to calm down before the next bird takes wing.

The summer of 1974 was a fairly dry one in Michigan,

and I had good gunning by hunting the streambeds and pond shores where the cover was higher and thicker, and the food more available. I didn't get many birds, mind you, but the ammo companies got rich off me. About two weeks after the season opened, the autumn rains came, and I found the birds to be back in their usual haunts on subsequent hunts.

The covers, themselves, are not quite so easy to define in terms of elements to be considered. The grouse arises as the sun strikes the treetops—a bit later on cloudy days—and goes to the nearest source of gravel. Being gallinaceous, the bird needs some grit in his crop to grind up the food he will take in that day.

From the road beds or gravel strip, he heads for feed: a grapevine tangle, a handy overgrown orchard, or any other area the bird will find sufficient food. At this time of year, the birds are found primarily in the aspen that is 8 to 15 years of age, and in any recently disturbed area, such as a burn or a clearcut area. A sunny hillside covered with mixed aspen and birch should never be passed up, and the edges are important.

Essentially, edge cover is wherever one type of vegetation changes to another type, like where aspen meets an open field, or where mature hardwoods merge into small species of trees such as cherry, or where bushes such as blackberry, mountain laurel and alder may occur—not together, of course.

The more edges there are, the better chance you have of finding grouse, because they are edge birds. When the Pilgrims landed, few grouse were present because of the expanses of unbroken, mature forest. Fires and land clearing created the edges, and the birds flourished. Today, as many small farms are driven out of business because of economic conditions, the pastured woodlot comes back with understory vegetation, and the birds come with it. Pastures are taken back over by plant succession, and eventually a pioneer forest evolves, and the grouse again inhabit the old family homestead.

As discussed earlier, in such conditions, it is easy to find grouse and woodcock together in combination covers. If the edge cover the grouse seeks is along a streambed that the 'cock are using for migration, then shooting can be fast and frustrating. All set for the whirr of grouse wings, a shooter can be caught off guard by the spiraling flush of a woodcock. It's like looking for a fastball and getting a knuckleball instead—and vice versa if you're sure the dog has a 'cock nailed and a grouse bores out low and fast.

Where the edge cover occurs away from established migrational routes for woodcock, then grouse are the best bet. If the edge cover is minimal, but a stream is nearby, the woodcock will be present, but not the grouse, unless it has been dry, as explained earlier. Knowing this, it is possible to do some exploration and set up a network of covers that contain either grouse, woodcock, or both.

For my part, I plead guilty to letting the grouse off the hook until the woodcock are gone from the northern climes, concentrating on that bounty while it is available. Once the 'cock have headed south for good, I turn all attention to the grouse.

Sometimes, even the fastball and knuckler aren't enough to consider. A few seasons back, I was working a good combination cover and had sacked three woodcock and a grouse— and missed at least that many shots. The dog pinned a bird near a small clump of multiflora rose, and as I approached, a gorgeous rooster pheasant hurtled out. I missed both barrels, and spent the rest of the time in that cover missing everything else because my mind had factored in the pheasant population. Naturally, I never saw another one.

Sometimes, the covers you hunt will be too easy, and therefore tough on the birds. For example, near my home there is an area of farmland with second-growth woodlots that are returning after being cut over 15 years ago. These returning woodlots have been perfect grouse cover, and the birds have flourished.

However, being surrounded by open farmland, the woodlots can be a deathtrap for grouse. A party of gunners can chase the same birds around inside a woodlot, and the birds will never leave, just flying back and forth from end to end. If a gunner is so moved, and has enough shells and daylight, he'll eventually bag every grouse in such a cover, merely be making enough tracks. Such shooting is unsportsmanlike and intolerable. I don't hunt these areas any more, but some of my acquaintances do, making one pass and then going to the next area. I see nothing wrong with this.

In a way, most grouse covers are like that; little islands of the proper type of cover and available food surrounded by vast areas of empty forest. These "pockets" are treasured by shooters, with good reason. Breathes there a soul so dead that wouldn't steal a good cover as his own if he thought he could get away with it?

Sexing and aging the grouse brought to bag is not really as easy as with woodcock. The young birds are overall smaller than the adults by about 5%. Being nonmigratory, they mature more slowly, and indeed are really not totally adult-sized until the gunning season is usually closed. Sadly, many of the birds taken at the beginning of the shooting season are little larger than good sized quail, particularly when the season opens early. But, an early opener helps scatter the family groups while thick, summer dense cover shields them.

Sexing is trickier than aging. There are various methods, all of which have exceptions that renders them less than reliable. Some say that the dark band on the fanlike tail is unbroken in color on males, and is broken on the two center tailfeathers with females. However, some males will have a broken band, particularly young birds.

Comparison of the breast coloration and dark "ruff" at the neck helps greatly. The male has a lighter breast feather coloration than the female, whose breast shows more distinct rusty colored mottling. In addition, the male has a distinct ruff, while the female has a very small one.

Like body size in woodcock, however, this works best if you have a bird of each sex in hand. The smaller female may resemble the larger male unless you've looked at a lot of grouse.

Instead, pluck a rump feather from the downed bird and examine it. The female's feather will have one white dot, the male's will have two. After experience, however, the overall larger size and darker ruff will quickly distinguish the male from the female at a glance.

Steve Smith

Prospecting for Grouse and Woodcock

The canoe grated to a halt on the tiny, wooded atoll in the broad, shallow river. The bird dog hopped gingerly from the bow, making a tiny splash at water's edge as she did. Loading our doubles, my gunning partner and I wordlessly separated and plunged into the still damp underbrush that covered the small island.

Stopped by the absence of a tinkling bell, I turned to my right, and there in a clearing in the center of the island stood the dog, locked up tightly on point, head and tail both high. Moving in to flush, I tripped over a downed log, and before I could right myself, I heard the twittering of a flushed woodcock, followed by a muffled crack from my partner's 20-gauge. Thus began a day of island hopping along that river in Michigan's Upper Peninsula, a day filled with similar results.

Hunting birds from a canoe or boat makes good sense. For example, in some of the sections of the Maritime Provinces of Canada, this is the way woodcock are hunted all the time. Partly because of inaccessibility by any other method, and partly because it's productive.

In the United States, the method still makes good sense and makes for good shooting. Let's look at the facts, as they say.

First of all, we have seen that woodcock use river valleys and streambeds as navigational aids and as ready supplies of food, this because of the invertebrates which inhabit the moist soils of such places. We have also seen that some of the best, indeed THE best woodcock covers are located at the confluence of streams—where a stream joins a larger river, or where a feeder creek enters. Birds from one river valley are funneled here from their summering grounds, and await favorable winds for migration.

Then it makes sense to hunt these river valleys and the adjoining covers nearby for woodcock. Naturally, there is no better way to hunt than by boat. I don't mean shooting from a boat, but using the craft—canoe, rowboat, or something similar—as a method of transportation from one likely cover to the next.

By doing so, a shooter can pick up a bird here, another there, and after a few miles of very pleasant floating on a river aflame with autumn color, he will have his limit.

Grouse, too, are highly susceptible to being hunted via the water route for another set of reasons. Rivers create edge cover—changing vegetation patterns, and as outlined earlier, dry years tend to concentrate grouse near water, and in low spots where the available moisture makes for thicker growing cover vegetation. This thicker cover also carries ample food for the birds, and places them at a disadvantage when being hunted from the water. How? When approached from the water's edge, the birds have a tendency to move away from the familiar streamside vegetation and they find themselves moving into increasingly thinner and thinner cover because of the lack of the water's influence on plant growth farther up the riverbed slope. Finally, they are forced to either fly across thin cover, and away from the familiar streamside haunts, or freeze in a patch of cover and hope you'll pass by. Now, you've got them. An open shot is not that difficult or rare in such circumstances.

The procedure, then, is for a pair of gunners to use a pair of vehicles to accomplish float tripping for grouse and woodcock. One vehicle is left downstream, and both buddies pile into the canoe-laden car that is left for the drive to the upstream put-in spot. A little experience will help you time your trips, but after awhile you just about know how long a float will take.

Floating downstream, and finishing the hunt, the canoe or boat is thrown on the waiting vehicle at a handy bridge or low spot on the riverbank, and the drive to take one partner to his upstream car is executed. There you are. The cars and the boat have been accounted for, and so have a few birds.

I make one of these trips about twice a year, and have come up with some things to make the trip more enjoyable. The number one rule is to make sure that the land you wish to hunt is open to you. One way, naturally, is to garner permission beforehand. The other way is to make sure that you choose a river with a lot of public land bordering it. In the Great Lakes states, this is not too difficult, and not really impossible anywhere.

A side benefit can be realized here. By hunting river valleys in this manner, on public land, you are able to get to places that car-conscious nimrods can't find or get to. Thus, you are actually able to have virgin covers to yourself.

On the Muskegon River, in Michigan's Lower Peninsula, there is one stretch of river that ambles 49 miles through state-owned land. Not a cabin, not a road, and only one bridge that is out of use crosses this stream during that entire 49-mile jaunt. It is pure heaven to hunt such covers, but it is a two-day affair, and then some. I like to start that trip on a Friday after work and end it on a Sunday evening. My parish priest is a bird hunter and understands. I'd take him with me, but he works weekends. By the way, you don't want to make such a trip alone—should you get an attack of appendicitis—it's damned lonely out there.

Last season I started packing a light flyrod and a handful of deer-hair flies with which to coax a few smallmouths from the river's many pools. Fall is a great time for good small-

mouth and trout action, and there is no streamside lunch better than bass or rainbow filets and breast of woodcock or
grouse over an open fire and topped off with a crackling white
wine, cooled in the rapids of that river.

Naturally, all canoeing rules apply. Make sure someone
knows where you are and when you're expected back. Keep
everything in double plastic bags, and carry lots of extra
clothing. Also, watch for the occasional mallard or woodduck
on the backwater pools if duck season is open. Float tripping is
a great way to beat the crowds, and it's lots easier on the legs
than walking to these covers.

Besides floating for grouse and woodcock, another
method or two I'd like to suggest can put you far from the
crowds and into productive grouse cover. One way is by
hunting the fire roads that crisscross state-owned land. These
roads are nothing more than twin tracks, or ruts, and many of
them haven't been used in so long that aspen and other pioneer plants are growing in ruts.

Grouse love to move out to these roads in early morning
and evening to scratch around. Also, on wet but clearing
mornings, the grouse will just come out and walk around until
the cover dries so that they can feed more comfortably.

At such times, walking along these roads can produce a
few birds. Some fellows even use binoculars to look down
stretches of road to try to spot a grouse first, but it really isn't
necessary. When you spy a grouse, you are able to approach
steadily and quietly because of the good footing. Most likely,
the bird will scurry into the roadside vegetation and freeze,
hoping you'll pass. Here, Old Fido can nail him solid, and you
get a shot. This type of shooting is even productive without a
dog because you've seen where the bird has entered the woods
from the road, and a little stop and go should put him up. It
doesn't always work, by the way, but what method does?

Another way that can lead to a weekend of enjoyable
gunning, and get you away from the crowds, is to backpack in
for grouse and woodcock. As the shooting season progresses,
covers that are handy and close to a road are often overshot by
parties of hunters. When this happens, the gunner must look

elsewhere. In Michigan, about half or even more of the available covers are never touched because they are too far from the roads, and can't be easily hunted without a lot of walking. Now, it makes little sense to hike for three hours to hunt one cover that may take 15 minutes to work, and then hike out. However, if a shooter can locate several or a half-dozen covers in close proximity to one another, the stage is set for a backpack trip in.

Carrying food, tent, cooking utensils and shotgun in is no easy feat, so restrict yourself to an hour's forced march at most. A sling on your gun helps substantially, and carrying dehydrated food cuts down on that weight.

Arriving at your predetermined site, set up camp and start hunting. This is fine for a weekend trip, and the area, naturally, should be scouted out beforehand—maybe on a summer hike.

There is one spot in northern Michigan that has the beginnings of several small streams, a flowing spring, and a good series of combination grouse and woodcock covers along these streams. They are too small to float, even if you lugged a canoe back there, but they are perfect for the backpacking bird hunter. A few essentials on the back, a pocket full of shells, a day or two with no pressing obligations, and you can have shooting pleasure all alone in such covers.

Finding spots such as this is easiest by using the aforementioned topographical maps issued by the U.S. Department of the Interior. These maps give land formations, indicate public land to a certain extent, and most importantly give indications of water—lakes, streams, bogs, marshes—and also elevation.

The elevation is indicated by interval lines, and these intervals vary, so use the map key. They also show houses and roads and other man-made features, but their real value is in showing land formations.

For example, one nice grouse cover I found lies on the edge of a large swamp in a county near my home. I found it by looking at a topo map. The cover adjoins the swamp, which is the only low spot and break among hundreds of acres of pine forest in the county. When looking for grouse cover, as stated earlier, look for edge cover. The drop in elevation as well as the key character for swamp told me the edge might exist there. I drove my four-wheel-drive as far as I could on a fire road and hiked the remaining mile or two into the cover, shot three grouse and hiked out—after getting lost a bit.

Another time, I located a dandy grouse and woodcock cover by going into a section of forested land looking for a small, intermittent stream, hoping to photograph some wild-flowers for an educational filmstrip I was producing. Intermittent streams are courses that only flow during high-water times, and are just well-vegetated valleys the rest of the year.

I was unlucky in finding the species of wildflower I sought, but found a species of grouse I was very familiar with. I marked this spot on the topo map with a grease pencil. Returning in the fall, I shot two grouse and a woodcock in less than hour. I visit this place only once a year, because it is so small and fragile, and it's a rough hike in, but I know I can always move birds there.

Topo maps are also helpful in finding deserted spots that may hold birds, such as old farmsteads and old logging towns. While trying to find the owner of a spot recorded on my circa 1965 topo map, I was informed by the local agriculture agent that the farm had been taken for back taxes several years earlier and hadn't been resold. I hustled to the place the map indicated, and found a beautiful little overgrown farm of about 80 acres now deserted.

The farmer had been unable to scratch a living from the sandy soil, and his buildings and fields were in a state of advanced plant succession. Where he once pastured his mild cattle, aspen and alders flourished. The little stream course I was seeking originally was a maze of alders and blackberry thickets. I shot a grouse and a woodcock, and missed thrice that number of each.

However, I really hit the mother lode when I found the remains of his old orchard. Scarcely a half-dozen trees stood clustered together, sagged by the weight of ripe Northern

Spies. I flushed four grouse from under the boughs, killing two and scaring hell out of the others. I filled my game bag with apples and left. I'll return this year.

Another time, the topo maps showed the existence of a tiny village with several dwellings. The name of the village escapes me now, but I asked around a northern town about it, and nobody could help me out.

Finally, an old farmer at the corner gas station told me that it had been a little farming community, but had gone under during the Great Depression in the 30's, and the state had taken it over for back taxes.

I located this ghost town, nestled in the hills of a rolling hardwood forest, and jumped a deer from in front of what had once been a filling station.

The only source of water was a small swamp and an intermittent stream, according to my map, and I passed by several farmhouses to get there, the Jeep bumping and grinding on the gravel road. I hunted the area out, and shot two woodcock and moved several grouse, but I couldn't wait to leave. I sensed a feeling of gloom there, and felt like an intruder. I shivered in the Jeep on the way out, despite the early November sunshine. I've never gone back and don't plan to for a while.

Topographic maps can also help you locate pockets of cover near civilization that may have been overlooked. These pockets are usually on farmland, and may take the form of woodlots or small swales the farmer can't plant and harvest properly, so he ignores them, and grouse and woodcock move in. A word of help here, though. These places will be no good unless there is an unbroken track of such spots back to a larger area of wilderness. Grouse and woodcock must have a constant touch with the wild, and cannot live where they are totally isolated. The topo maps will tell you if these places are of that type.

Whenever I go off on such prospecting forays, I make it a point to carry a compass and a supply of matches, as well as a candy bar or two. One of the best grouse covers I ever found was located while in the process of being lost, and I had great shooting. I never was able to locate it since then, although I've looked many times. Maybe someday.

II

When a grouse is about four months old, a sudden and strange urge permeates him, and he has the urge to be gone, to be off. This happens in the autumn, and well could be related to the shortening days. Males travel farther than females, probably hoping to find new, unoccupied areas to strut and drum.

In any event, the birds disperse from where they were hatched to new grounds, and inbreeding is prevented and new areas are populated by the fiercely territorial males and the females. This is the mystical "Fall Shuffle."

For the hunter, the fall shuffle is a real treat. Many birds can be flushed quickly, and the grouse are sometimes in the right spot for the hunter—the wrong spot for the grouse. As a result, many a naive young grouse ends up surrounded by wild rice because he happened to shuffle the wrong way.

The fall shuffle is also a time of losses by accident. Grouse fly into wires, houses, windows or in front of automobiles, and that's that. Many more survive and, perhaps genetically superior, they breed other survivors. For the hunter out prospecting for grouse, the fall shuffle—usually in early October—is a time of plenty.

Now, a strange thing about grouse physiology and the fall shuffle can conspire to give the shooter some fine action in the early fall. A little topography accentuates the whole process, and the result is a high number of flushes in some unlikely grouse cover. To see how this works, let's anthropomorphize for a bit, pretend we're a grouse, and see what happens.

Here you are, content to be in the old, familiar, home covers. Mother Grouse no longer hovers over you and protects you. You've grown to nearly adult size through the lazy summer, growing fat and a bit sassy on the berries and plentiful fruits.

Now as the days grow short, an unfamiliar urge grabs you and you suddenly want to see what's on the other side of the hill, so you take off walking. Small streams and open areas of a few acres are crossed with a few strong wingbeats, and the journey to wherever continues. The frosty nights and the flaming maples only hurry you on your way faster. You know that you want to be at wherever that place is quickly—why, you're still a little foggy about.

A few days after you begin, you encounter a wide lake, or perhaps a vast open meadow, or maybe a swamp too wet to walk across. Regardless, the area can't be negotiated on foot, and it's too far to fly. Your wings have never failed you before, but now you sense that the mile-wide expanse of unwalkable terrain is too much for your short, strong appendages.

To make things worse, the area that you've chosen is really not all that great as far as cover is concerned. True, there are some bushes and shrubs near the barrier, but they offer only small bits of concealment. You feel nervous, but you know your destiny is across the wide expanse, so you wait, unsure of what to do.

One day, as you wait, a tinkling of a bell grows closer. A dog's form materializes, followed by a man. You look for cover, hunkering down in the pitiful depression where once a spruce stood, but was toppled by the wind. The dog gets closer and suddenly stiffens, looking at you. The man moves in and you panic. Your wings are like thunder in the stillness. The man raises his shotgun. . . . .

This is the case of a bird being taken, by chance, from an area where it had no right being. The barrier phenomenon is well known to some grouse hunters, and completely foreign to others.

Boiled down, all it says is this: Grouse shuffle out in the fall to establish and populate new areas. Some of the shuffling grouse will come against a barrier that is too wide to fly across and too wet or unsafe to walk across. So, the young, inexperienced birds wait. They usually don't have to wait very long. The cover near the barrier is not usually that good, and the birds are picked off by any of the predators such as hawks or owls.

The smart hunter, knowing this, will often concentrate his

hunting to areas around lakes and swamps where the birds are likely to be held back by the barrier. The western and northern edges seem to be the best for this, for some reason, perhaps because of thicker vegetative growth due to sunlight. In any event, the grouse that are so trapped are doomed. Either the winged or two-footed hunter will have them for a meal. Shooting such birds does not harm, apparently, the population. These birds are not the chosen survivors. Rather, they are the expendable ones, the ones that have been selected against by luck or genes or whatever. They are the losers. The clever grouse hunter will be there to cash in.

Steve Smith

After Dark

The twilight flight of woodcock from the day's resting place to the nighttime feeding grounds is called "dusking." I've sort of picked up the same kind of habit—but for different reasons. My feeding tastes are not quite those of the woodcock but we seem to share certain instincts.

I like to walk away from the problems of the day come evening time and make my way back home in the growing dark. This is the soft part of the day, and the wash of oncoming night has a calming touch. There's a special comfort standing in the meadow while pheasant glide down around me to roost. The cackle of satisfaction as they find a favorite spot is about the last of the daylight sounds around here, and after a few exchanges of gossip and bragging, they settle down to sleep, pausing, no doubt, as I do, to be lulled into whatever dreams they dream by the tenor of peepers and the basso profundo of bullfrogs.

As the one world takes over from the other under starlight I am convoyed by owls impatient for me to be on my way and leave them to their sifting of the field. Silver threads are stitched by muskrats across the surface of the pond. A largemouth bass bullies his way through a school of shiners and a pair of mallards indignantly sculls away across the pond to get to the far side of me. An owl recites, "Who cooks for you, who cooks for you?" as I walk the last few minutes homeward to my own supper, leaving the late diners alone outside to gather theirs.

Somehow, still reluctant to leave the dark things to their

night, I stand and wait to take just one more piece of quiet with me—something that I can carry on to bed to use as an anchor against the coming of the day, soothing sound to carry in the chamber of my ear. But there is to be no sweet lullaby this night. Instead, the flinty barking of a fox chips away the softness of the moment—cold reminder, added to the owl, that there are few who ever sleep an uninterrupted sleep more than once.

Gene Hill

A South
Seas Bird

I was having lunch with a friend, let's call him George, at one of those topless restaurants in California, when for some reason he suddenly remembered that he wanted to get a new recoil pad fitted on his 20-gauge side-by-side. A while later when we were in the car headed for Pachmayr Gun Works, I remarked to George that he seemed to have nothing but guns and shooting on his mind and mentioned the old "all work and no play" adage. To further the point, I told him the story about the avid birdshooter who had sort of been dragooned into serving as part of the crew (between seasons, of course) on one of those Pacific sailing races.

They hadn't been out too long when a terrific storm came up and our friend was washed overboard. When he came to, he found he was on a lovely island and an exquisite young girl was offering him a mixture of rum and coconut milk to help restore his senses. As soon as she saw him recovering she ran off into the lush jungle but quickly returned with some cold remains of what had been a succulent roasted pig. Now, all his senses restored, he began to sit up and take notice of his surroundings. He couldn't help but notice the young lady was as scantily clad as she was beautiful. Then she rolled over to him, cradled his head in her arms and whispered "Strange man . . . before someone comes to rescue you, you and I are going to a secret place and I will make you very happy, but you must promise never to tell a soul."

Then she smiled again, the fragrance of her skin flooding his senses and said, "Do you know what I mean?"

"You bet I do," he said, "you've got woodcock shooting on this island and I'll never tell anybody!"

George thought about the story for a minute, narrowly avoiding an old lady with orange hair driving a Sting Ray, and said, "She must have been mistaken . . . there is a Pacific *snipe* that looks a little like a woodcock but . . ."

                                                              Gene Hill

Take Time
To Smile

As the readers of this book are no doubt aware, grouse and woodcock hunters are a cut above the average human, given to quoting Shakespeare, donating to the local opera company, and supporting the work of struggling young artists. Comparing them to pheasant hunters is like comparing the finest imported scotch with a can of beer.

Come, then, on a typical woodcock hunt with two such sterling personages to watch the drama of the chase unfold in all its magnificent splendor.

The time is mid-October, the season of the gods. The place, Michigan's Lower Peninsula—some of the best ruffed grouse and woodcock territory found anywhere on the planet. The cast of characters include Mark Sutton (M), his pointer, Dinah (known as Dog) and myself. I have chosen to record this episode just as it happened, with no attempt to embellish. I let the record stand for itself. All events are true, with times noted for verification purposes.

6:02 A.M.—M arrives at house driving his shooting car. Name of vehicle is derived from condition of clutch, engine, and transmission, all of which are, indeed, shot. Car—a 1954 Chevy—awakens several neighbors because it has not seen a muffler since the spring of 1959.

6:05 A.M.—Dog bounds from car and evacuates on Self's prize roses. M chuckles good naturedly at the antics of his animal, while Self calls down wrath of gods on both M and his playful compadre. With this ritual completed, all leave for the northern Michigan shooting grounds.

7:15 A.M.—Arriving at first cover of the day, we disembark from car. Our clothes carry the odor of exhaust fumes from the shooting car. Self promptly closes thumb in breech of fine, side-by-side 20-gauge double. M laughs with such enthusiasm that standing upright becomes impossible for him, and I take solace in the fact that M is now wet from rolling convulsively in the frosty grass. I curse the immortal soul of M for such frivolity. For good measure, I also curse 20-gauge.

8:12 A.M.—After missing four straight woodcock and a grouse, I finally connect on a rising woodcock. Dog, which has flawlessly retrieved all three of M's 'birds (taken with three shots), calmly finds and eats this bird, including head and bill. I am wild with rage; M is wild with hysteria brought on by inability to take in oxygen fast enough to support peals of laughter. I curse Dog with vocabulary usually reserved for Nazi war criminals and child molesters. Dog licks chops and eagerly demands that we continue hunt.

9:27 A.M.—While attempting crossing of drainage ditch via rotting log—with advice of myself, M executes perfect two-and-a-half gainer from the tuck position off said log and into ditch. Being the only available judges, Dog and I score dive at a 7.5, no degree of difficulty. M emerges from ditch encrusted with mud, pouring water from gun barrels. Using camera I keep for such occasions, I record incident for posterity. M curses ditch, log, Self, and Nikon camera company.

10:04 A.M.—Spying a grouse perched in an apple tree, M, Self, and Dog stalk nearer in anticipation of shooting when grouse flushes. Grouse chooses to remain in tree, sensing we will not fire at perched bird. What grouse does not know is that he is safe in flying, because we are lousy shots. Regardless, attempts at hurling sticks, stones, apples, and expletives fail to dislodge bird. M finally moves closer to shake low-hanging limb.

Grouse chooses this instant to release three-days' worth of solid excrement onto M's hat brim. M calls grouse names that I have not heard since working on the docks between college semesters. Grouse knows an insult when he hears it, and flaps away. Four shots ring out, and grouse continues unscathed to land in nearby apple tree. We do not follow: M is too angry, and I cannot see clearly due to tear-shrouded vision.

11:42 A.M.—As midday approaches, we drive into nearest town to get some lunch at a diner called "Mom's." Mom is in attendance and bars M's entry, citing color and odor of M's clothing from recent excursion into ditch. M points out that this odor would be a marked improvement over smells emanating from Mom's kitchen. Mom orders M out, but I stay to order two cheeseburgers to go. Arriving back at the shooting car, I toss M's burger to him from passenger's seat. Dog, leaning over from the back seat, picks off burger with ease of an NFL flanker, and burger promptly joins my woodcock in Dog's digestive tract. M uses words I've never heard before to describe Dog, her gastronomical gymnastics, and her preceding three generations.

12:08 P.M.—We drive to next cover dubbed the "Old Homestead," so named as M located old basement two seasons ago. Unfortunately M determined it was a basement from the horizontal position looking up. Dog points a woodcock at base of birch clump. I miss both barrels, but make dog look for nonexistent bird. M and Dog both claim I am liar. They are, of course, correct.

12:43 P.M.—By foot, we investigate "Wild Boar" cover, so named because five years ago Dog pointed a sow and six suckling pigs in a patch of blackberry vines, a feat I remind M of on each visit of the last five years. M claims woodcock are on hillside; I claim they are in swamp. Dog points woodcock in half-picked cornfield while we argue. M runs over and shoots bird, which Dog intends to eat to tamp down snack of previous woodcock and burger. Fight ensues. M wrestles dog amongst cornstalks, emerging victorious, even though I offer advice to Dog. I am laughing until my sides ache as M curses Dog, Me, and what is left of woodcock. We leave this cover.

1:04 P.M.—Arriving at the Pasture Cover, we ask permission to hunt from crusty old farmer. We are never denied such permission because sadistic farmer enjoys watching city hunters try to negotiate 40-acre pasture to gain access to a five-acre patch of alders and aspen located in center of pasture. Pasture is indisputable domain of an Angus bull with the disposition of Adolph Eichmann, and the physical attributes of average-sized GMC tractor.

1:10 P.M.—Chase is joined, as Bull spots our intrusion. We break for the cover, and Bull makes for M, who is slowed by mud-encrusted clothing, *vis-à-vis* the ditch at 9:27 A.M. As I pound for safety of the patch of cover, it occurs to me that Bull especially hates M and would gladly swear off heifers and trundle up south face of Matterhorn for one decent shot at M. Obviously, Bull is perceptive creature, and my estimation of this animal grows. Under pressure, M has open field moves like O. J. Simpson, and we gain the safety of the cover one half-second ahead of 1½ tons of black fury.

1:12 P.M.—Knowing the routine by rote, Bull ambles to the end of the cover to await our arrival. We hunt out the cover, and move no birds. Spotting Bull at the end of the cover, we caucus to plan strategy about the time the skies open up with monsoon-like deluge. We decide that Bull will grow weary of waiting in the rain, and retire from the field of combat for safety of barn. Glancing at barn, we notice that farmer has invited over neighbors who have set up lawn chairs under eaves of that building to witness drama, and crowd sentiments are running for Bull.

2:43 P.M.—Unable to stand rain any longer, and seeing that Bull means to wait us out, we elect to make a run for it. M breaks left, I head right, aiming for safety of barnyard. Wild cheer goes up from the crowd. Cleansed of mud, M stretches out lead over Bull, who switches targets and comes for me.

2:45 P.M.—Bull is gaining as my temples throb from exertion and breathing becomes shallow and labored. Safety beyond electric fence beckons invitingly, and I am verbally encouraged by M, who has already gained safety. Bull is verbally encouraged by occupants of barn. Leaping over electric fence, I miscalculate my ability, wet footing, and fence's height, coming down astraddle it. My clothes are wet; juice is on. I curse Bull, farmer, fence, and Benjamin Franklin. Bull takes out frustrations on my hunting hat, dropped at midpoint of latest dash. Cheers from the barn.

2:50 P.M.—Thoroughly bushed, we head home, thankful for the chance to be outdoors on such a glorious day.

One of the toughest things about grouse and woodcock hunting, to those who have been thoroughly indoctrinated in the sport, is to find covers that are productive, of the right age, offer fairly decent shooting, and PRIVATE.

Everybody knows that keeping a cover secret is a chore, and jokes about blindfolding people before they are taken into a good one are often cruelly truthful. There are ways to make sure that a casual acquaintance never returns to a cover with HIS buddies, but they are illegal in every state and province, and also violate the odd Commandment or two.

Naturally, there are devious ways that covers can be masked, newcomers can be discouraged from interloping, and slightly known shooters from your gun club can be misled. However, the main way to guarantee your private shooting in your private covers—without interference—is to learn how to tell lies.

Not knowing how, exactly, I contacted a few friends who number among their faults the sport of fishing. Everybody knows that the hook and line set has taken the science of lieing and honed it to an art form, so I figured this was the place to start.

From what they told me, the lies fall into certain categories. First off, there's the kind that has to be told to the wives of the guilty so that they can get to go hunting in the first place. This type of lie usually centers around two or three basic premises. Premise number one is that the bigger the lie, the more believable it is. Instead of telling the little woman you're going hunting, tell her that you are doing field research at the request of the local fish and game department, that only a man of your expertise would suffice, and you had to be gone every Saturday during the season to help in this important work.

With a little ingenuity, you could produce an official looking letter on government stationery to back up your claims. A friend of mine, a superintendent of schools, uses this ruse to go fishing. It's been working for years for him.

Another way involves the use of the hunting buddy to substantiate your claim to hunting freedom. Get the other guy to feign an illness, something terminal but rare. Note that the guy is sensitive about his condition, but the prognosis is not good. Then, tell the little woman that you are going to do everything in your power to make sure that he gets as much sport as possible before the Grim Reaper makes his call on your ailing conspirator. Naturally, your wife will agree 100%, and will insist that you even use the vacation time you've saved to visit Grandmother Fishbait in the summer to go hunting. Have the "illness" linger so you can parlay this into several season's worth of sport. When the wife gets suspicious, claim a miracle cure, and think of something else.

Scientists and anthropologists tell us that the feelings we experience during the autumn months are genetically remembered feelings of migration that our ancestors had when the herds that fed them started the fall movement to winter pasture. When the herds moved, we moved, and this autumn restlessness is with us yet today, even though we are a "civilized" species.

If the grouse and woodcock hunter has an urge to be up and gone when the sun's rays slant just so, the man's wife usually has an urge to clean up the family cave, like her long ago, long vanished Neanderthal sister.

To the shooter, this is not the situation one would hope for. In truth, no two people can look at a situation and see it entirely the same. That is why we need diplomats, judges, and referees. Wives definitely don't look at things the way we do.

Where a weather forecast of morning fog but clearing in the afternoon gives you and me thoughts of ideal scenting conditions for our dogs, Sweetwife is liable to think in terms of cleaning the garage for winter, washing the windows, or— horror of horrors—putting up storm windows.

The hunter, then, must be fast on his feet to keep one step ahead. That is why I will pass along a few excuses that I have used successfully over the years to free myself from the domestic drivel that keeps me from the covers I love so much.

One of the best is what I call the "Look-At-All-The-Things-I-Don't-Do" gambit. By pointing out that you don't bowl, play poker, shoot pool in some den of ill repute which serves distilled spirits, or shoot skeet, you can make yourself look put-upon and deserving of just this little pleasure. If you do any or all of the above, point out that you are not a heroin addict, even though it would most likely end up cheaper in the long run.

Naturally, you now have the tacit agreement of your mate that you are deserving of a few mornings out, say 40 or 50, during season.

Another one I've found helpful is the "Stick and Carrot Routine." In this excuse, the hunter promises to do some long-waiting repair project around home right after he returns from hunting. Talk glowingly about the placement of that painting Aunt Agatha gave you for Christmas last year, or discuss minutiae about the new shower door you've promised to put up. When you return from hunting, act brave, but let a small limp creep into your walk, and try—unsuccessfully, of course—to hide a grimace of pain from that old football injury. Naturally, the little woman takes pity on you and you're off the well-known hook.

The third in this series of excuses might be called the "Team Approach," or more correctly the "Secret Weapon." This one takes a little timing, but never fails.

At a time in the afternoon that you think is exactly right, just mention that you don't think you'll go woodcock hunting tomorrow, because you have a lot to do around the house. Mention that you haven't been home much on the weekends lately—ignoring her retort that "at all" could be substituted for "much." Then, let the subject drop. Wife is now in a state of euphoria. All looks right with the world through her eyes. This is the state of mind that you want her in.

At a prearranged time, your grouse and woodcocking pal phones you. You make sure that the whole house hears your end of the conversation in which you loudly defend your right to stay home this Saturday. You announce that Mom and the kiddies are more important to you this weekend, and that you are not wasting another weekend stomping through scratchy cover. Shock is now added to your wife's store of felt emotions.

Slamming the receiver down, you hotly question why YOU always have to be the one to go hunting with that guy. Is it your fault that the other guy's wife won't let him out of the house save this one day? Is it YOUR fault that he has no other friends on this orb and that he is in a state of suicidal depression from which only YOU can save him? So what if the character IS the godfather of your firstborn, right is right!

By now, Wife is in tears, and she demands that you phone back—nay, she insists—that you make peace. You resist, asking why a friendship which has lasted since the third grade should have anything to do with hunting? You finally relent, and at Wife's bidding, offer to go hunting as a truce offering between old friends. She is flushed with victory and a feeling of Christian peacemaking; you surrender in abject silence. Excusing yourself to go buy a pouch of tobacco, you stop at the nearest phone booth to repeat the opposite end of the scenario so that your buddy can spring free too.

All of the preceding goes to prove that grouse and woodcock hunters enjoy their sport to the utmost, derive the greatest pleasure from the little things, and have to be damned fast on their feet!

The other types of lies the hunter must learn to tell are the kinds involving the hiding of covers from the prying eyes of other similarly smitten shooters. Hiding the car near the cover does no good, neither does sweeping out tire tracks on a dirt road. Masking the direction of the covers works on only the most obtuse, so the old-fashioned fib works best.

In reverse of the usual fisherman's gambit, it is best to always maintain that you shoot almost no birds whatsoever. Spend a lot of time griping about the phases of the moon, quizzing the other guy about HIS covers, and suggesting that you may just pack it in and go to New Brunswick, hire a guide, and take your shooting there, and to hell with the local stuff.

Naturally, anybody listening to your litany will figure you are really a slouch as a hunter, and will cross you off. In addition, some poor slob may even take pity on you and invite you along to one of his covers. You now have added another one to your list (provided you hunt on days you know he doesn't) and you've divulged none of your own.

Another way to hide your woodcock covers is to take a few birds you've shot to the gun club to give them away. Ask the woodcock hunters there to identify the birds for you, give them to him because you hate the taste, and talk glowingly about the prospects of great duck or pheasant shooting. Now, nobody but a polygraph expert can uncover your secret.

If keeping the covers secret is a chore, covering up your own ineptitude with a smoothbore is even worse. You are not dealing with strangers here, but with people who know both you and your abilities, so a fresh stock of lies about why you missed are in order before each season begins.

I admire the fellow who can miss both barrels at a going away bird, laugh at himself, and shrug off the experience. I fight waves of nausea with each missed shell, and even if I connect, if the gun were not mounted just so, or I got lucky, I'm concerned. I don't want "lucky." I want "good." Most days I'll settle for lucky.

Knowing this, how do you mask your misses under a believable barrage of verbiage? Well, to start off with, you have to be willing to admit, about once every two trips, that you really did miss for no good reason. Then your excuses will be better accepted when you do use them. It's the old case of crying "wolf" too many times and not being believed.

Then, as far as excuses go, the best way is to divide these into several categories and go from there, rotating categories as the situation permits.

One category is the faulty equipment bracket. Wearing the wrong type of clothing makes you uncomfortable in a woodcock and grouse cover, so blame the clothing for a miss. The coat binds, the pants weren't thick enough to turn the briars, and so on. BUT, make sure that you do the complaining before you ever get into the cover. If you wait until you miss before making excuses, it'll sound like you're making excuses.

You can fudge on this category a bit too. If you miss a bird, quickly pull an empty shell from your pocket that is at least 15 years old—the old paper kind with the top wad—and blame the ammunition. Make sure your partner does not see you take the real empty from your gun.

Another way is to blame the gun. Once, I missed a wide open grouse with the first barrel at 20 yards—straight away! I was shocked to the point that I didn't even fire the second barrel. Instead, I got busy formulating an excuse. Thinking quickly, I pushed the release lever on the forearm, and claimed I hadn't assembled the gun correctiy, and when throwing up the piece to shoot, it had come apart. My companion bought it—until someone reads this to him.

Sometimes you can have a miss make you look like an expert. Claim that you missed because the bird was so close you were trying to shoot it with the edge of your pattern, and cuss glowingly. Partner walks away muttering "Edge of the pattern, I can't hit 'em with the whole damned thing!" You look good, he feels like a chump, which is the way it should be.

Naturally, the thick vegetation that grouse and woodcock inhabit is good for excuses aplenty. When you miss one, pick up a piece of deadfall off the ground. Hold it up so partner can see it, and lie through your teeth about how you just put your whole load into that branch instead of the bird. Partner thinks, now, that you would undoubtedly have scored except for cruel fate and the limb.

Another way is to bring along a pair of badly scratched

shooting glasses, even with large gaping cracks. Make a big production of showing these off before you actually start hunting. Tell him that even though you can hardly see through them, you'll wear them anyway because you value your eyesight. Once in the cover, switch glasses. If you miss, you've got your excuse. If you hit, you can point out what a great shot you are, being able to score even with such crummy optics. Remember to switch back before partner sees you again.

Lastly, try a variation of the "War wound" technique. Claiming an old injury, pick the easiest routes through the cover, making partner play dog. This puts you in the best position for a shot, and if you make it, again you look a cut above the average, what with your bad health and all.

Looking for excuses to buy new and expensive goodies for hunting comes a bit harder. New guns can be sneaked in and out, but things like four-wheel-drive vehicles are a little more tricky. Point out that you've had it with your wife having to drive the kids to school through deep snow, and you worry about her in that little imported tin can because of the crash factor in such a small vehicle. Tell her it's hers, and "borrow" it during season. She'll love it.

Once your excuse bag is full, you'll need some other finer points of grouse and woodcock hunting to make your day complete. One of these fine points is the art of falling down in a cover.

Now, sooner or later, you are going to take a dive in a cover. Most that I hunt are so thick that even if you fall you'll never hit the ground. But for the purposes of enlightenment, we should know how to fall, and how to categorize these falls.

The first type of fall is what I call the Cape Buffalo, or the "stick trick." In this one, the toe of one foot strikes a small limb or branch on the ground. In lifting that foot, the branch lifts, the opposite end embeds itself in the ground, and the foot cannot come down. Forward momentum takes over, and the laws of physics enter the picture in that a solid body with mass cannot be suspended at the horizontal for any length of time before gravity reaches up and grabs it.

When this happens, the stickee places his other foot

down farther ahead of where it should have been, the next step is even longer, and soon we are getting to see the cover at a speed associated with a taxiing jetliner. Naturally, the end result is to go face first to the forest floor. To execute this one correctly, one must look for the proper object on which to land. Since much of my woodcock hunting is done near cattle pastures, I usually emerge from the cover at the speed of an untamed juggernaut and tour the pasture. I'll leave it to your imagination about where I usually end up coming down. Degree of difficulty, 1.7.

Another type of fall is called the "Deadfall Dawdle." This one happens when the shooter decides to cross over a downed tree, brush pile, or what you have. Once atop the deadfall, be sure to stop to scan the horizon, or look for the dog. The laws of biology governing decaying vegetation in the temperate zone will take over, guaranteeing that the key limb in the pile will give way at this point, and you'll plunge earthward like the trap door on a gallows has been opened. To have this fall count, you must be unable to emerge from the downfall for at least 15 minutes. Degree of difficulty, 2.5.

A third type of fall commonly used is the "Mossy Rock Shuffle." This one is executed when crossing streams, rivers, or ditches in woodcock cover. Naturally, wishing to remain dry, we choose the path across that has the best series of rocks to use as, well, stepping stones. Pick out the kind covered with the algae known as spirogyra, as this is the most slippery. When one foot hits the slippery rock, it will fly out from under you, and is replaced by the other foot. When this one also flips skyward, the first foot is back for a second turn. The end on this fall comes when both feet are pointed at the heavens at the same time, and the splash in the closest, deepest pool takes place. Degree of difficulty, 2.5. Extra points for keeping the action going for longer than 30 seconds, and for all trout scared to death by your entry into the aforementioned pool. Real pros get extra points for eye-bulging, mouth gaping, and shotgun losing.

The last type of tumble takes concentration and teamwork. This is the "Pothole Plunge," and takes place under tightly controlled conditions. The conditions are: the dog is on point, it is obviously your shot, the cover is open, and there is nothing to distract you from shooting and scoring. You advance slowly, the dog steady. Just as you hear the bird flush, you step into a depression in the ground left by the roots of an overturned tree, long since decayed. Naturally, you get the same feeling as when you are walking down a flight of steps reading the paper, think there are no more steps and there are. You disappear from view, the bird flushes, you can't even see it to shoot. Partner is convulsed with glee. Degree of difficulty, 3.0. Extra points if the dog had a double pinned, and they both flew straightaway, side by side—your one chance of the season for a double.

If you can pin down the odd yuk or two from the things that happen naturally, what about the contrived situation? In other words, what about the Practical Joke? Certainly, this piece of Americana can be used to spice up a day when the birds just can't be located, or when the weather is just too miserable to get serious about the whole thing. Practical joking can take many forms, and my kid brother, Eric, is perhaps the greatest PJ'er presently in captivity. What he hasn't done to punch up a hunting trip already will no doubt be done this season—he has a new bag of them every year, and I always tumble.

For example, I like a cup of coffee about midmorning, and carry a thermos (when I remember it) for the purpose. Two years ago, last Christmas, Eric presented me, amid solemn fanfare, a nice white coffee mug with my name on it, and a picture of a flighting woodcock hand painted on the other side. I was thrilled. I should have saved my thrills. The next fall, I decided to initiate the cup on the drive up to the first cover on opening day. I was all alone, and whistling contendedly to myself. Steering the Jeep with my knee, I poured myself a steaming portion in the gift mug. As I savored the early morning coffee, I suddenly had sharp pains, as if my thighs were on fire, and a peculiar wet feeling penetrated my lap. Seems Kid Brother had drilled a small hole in the bottom of the cup and sealed it with paraffin wax. As the coffee heated the wax, it melted, and the coffee leaked out. There I was—55 miles an hour and cup resembling the hull of the Titanic. Plenty of yuks—for Eric.

Another time, he gave me a half dozen handloaded 20-gauge shells he wanted me to try. He sort of casually dumped them as a handful into my shooting vest pocket, and said no more about them. I should have smelled a rat, but didn't.

Along about noon, he and I got into a good concentration of 'cock, and we both shot quite a few shells. I'd run out of skeet loads, and then remembered the gift shells—the "special handloads." As the dog came on point, I groped frantically for the shells Eric had given me. My screams of dismay flushed the bird and set Eric into peals of gaiety. Seems he'd used some of the new, super adhesive glue now marketed to glue the brass ends of the shells into one huge mass. I couldn't tear even one loose to jam into my empty double. He finished shooting that cover alone. I tagged along behind and muttered black oaths concerning modern technology and kid brothers.

Just this past season, he pulled the ultimate PJ, the one from which I'm still trying to recover. For years, a small parcel of land that has a superb cover on it has been for sale by a downstate landowner. I'd always had permission to hunt this choice little corner, provided it never was sold. I happened to mention this to Eric once. Bad mistake. The rat ran out and bought signs which read "sold" and plastered them all over the cover. I stayed away from the cover, cursing the fates and real estate agents in general until his wife spilled the beans on him. I missed great shooting there all season. But did the cover go untouched? No. Eric hunted it when I wasn't around!

This year, I've got a few tricks planned myself. These will make the keepers of Stalag 7 look like choirboys. In any event, grouse and woodcock hunting certainly brings out the creative tendencies among its followers—something few other sports can do.

Speaking of creativity, with a little intellectual gymnastics, it's possible to actually make a few bucks from our Rich

Uncle—Sam—by grouse and woodcock hunting. Witness the following account.

TO: Internal Revenue Service Auditor
FROM: Steven R. Smith
RE: IRS query about item on form 1040 regarding deduction for business expenses. To wit: $13,050.40 for one pound of woodcock.

Dear Sir:
This letter will explain, I hope, the question that your office raised about the amount of $13,050.40 for a pound of woodcock. I took this as a legitimate business deduction because I often write about hunting and I was under the impression that expenses incurred that way are deductible.

You seemed to be most interested in how a pound of woodcock meat could cost such a sizeable sum of money. Well, in answer to your registered letter of 17 April this year, no—I didn't outright buy the meat for this amount. The purchase of wild meat is illegal. Instead, I arrived at this business deduction through a rather convoluted manner. I respectfully request that you sharpen your pencil, sit up straight, and try to follow as the story unfolds. . . . . .

It all started when I got an assignment to do a fall hunting article about woodcock for a magazine. Woodcock, you see, are little birds that live in the Northern tier of states, migrating southward during the autumn months. To fulfill the assignment, I'd have to bag three woodcock to have enough of them to photograph for the magazine article. At the average weight of woodcock, the three would total about one pound.

I started off quite innocently, figuring that I'd just sally forth with my full-choked 12-gauge pump gun, reasoning that if it would kill ducks it'd be just dandy on woodcock. Quite wrong, as it turns out. After missing about 40 of the little rascals, I gradually got the idea that something a little lighter and more open-choked was in order. I bought a 20-gauge side-by-side shotgun at a cost of $600 with which to shoot my pound of woodcock flesh (you guys at the IRS are no doubt familiar with the term "pound of flesh"). I've enclosed a copy of the bill of sale.

I soon found out that having the right shotgun wasn't the answer altogether. I still couldn't hit the birds because I had no warning that they were anywhere about until one would suddenly flutter up in my face.

Then, someone told me about a dog that would actually stand real stiff and "point" (with his nose) at a hiding woodcock. Naturally, my work required such a dog, so I bought one—already trained—for $500. The bill of sale is enclosed along with the bills for vet fees, food, and my neighbor's shrubbery. That's the extra $249.55 you see there under the section headed "DOG" on the attached financial explanation sheet.

About the time I got the dog business sorted out, I was ready to go bag my woodcock, write my magazine story, and pay my taxes on the income, like a normal American Patriot. But, another curve in the road. It seems the woodcock had been heavily hunted in my area, and the only place that held any of the birds was in a remote, swampy area far from the beaten tracks of blacktop highways.

Since walking through miles of swampland is about as appealing as pulling one's own teeth, I decided that for the sake of expediency and to get the magazine job done, I'd have to have some other means of transportation than my 1967 Chevy. That conclusion will explain, I believe, the $6,800 deduction under "JEEP" found on the attached sheet. Being a good American, I didn't even add the costs of gas, oil, insurance and so forth. I did, however, add one item that was related.

Shortly after the purchase of the Jeep, I found out that the so-called "swampy area" was in reality a place honeycombed with quicksand bogs. That will explain the $200 deduction for "TOWING" on the attached sheet. (See enclosed wire service clipping and photo for verification. That's me, there, the muddy one standing next to the roof of the Jeep. You wouldn't think so many people could gather in such a remote spot to gawk at another's misfortune, would you?)

Now by this time you must be wondering about the items marked LA., SN. LEG., and JOE. Let me explain. By the time I had my new gun, and new dog and new Jeep and was finally ready to gather my pound of woodcock, it became obvious that the critters had migrated south to the wintering grounds.

A little research told me that these wintering grounds were in Louisiana (LA.) so I loaded up the Jeep and headed off after them, hence the deduction of $1,100 for four days in Louisiana you see there on the by now-familiar sheet.

The diversity of wildlife in that state is staggering, as you may be aware. Among the more exciting species are rattle-snakes and cottonmouths, so I bought a set of snake leggings (SN. LEG.) and hired a guy named Joe (JOE) to guide me toward the woodcock and away from the snakes. Joe did neither very well, and I only got one woodcock.

Thanks to the snake leggings ($39.95) and Joe ($150) I managed to run afoul of some snakes with minimal results except to my cardiovascular system. That, of course, accounts for the $45 deduction for "VALIUM" so marked on the sheet.

Returning north with my one woodcock, now frozen to preserve it, I waited through a long winter, spring and summer for the next gunning season. Not wanting to waste the time, I decided to improve my shooting and dog handling skills. This will explain the section marked "MEMBERSHIPS—$200." Among these were two gun clubs, a field trial association, the Ruffed Grouse Society and another one I've forgotten.

In addition, I did research on the bird by questioning known woodcock hunters. Since most known woodcock hunters are best questioned after being plied with liberal amounts of a liquid known as "Jack Daniels," that will explain the $224 deduction for "RESEARCH EXPENSES."

By the time the next gunning season rolled around, I was ready. I'd even managed to find the location of a choice woodcock cover *vis-à-vis* the Jack Daniels deduction (see above).

The problem here was that my information was slightly faulty. A more suspicious person than I would think the omission of certain pertinent facts was deliberate, but that's another story. It seems the wonderful cover I'd located was in the middle of a large pasture presided over by a Hereford bull of prodigious proportions. An aged but determined specimen, the bull gave chase as soon as I entered the pasture. Naturally, I ran and the bull followed. The farmer kept screaming something about the red shooting vest, but it was hard to understand him as my breath was getting ragged and he was convulsed with laughter most of the time.

I think it was on the third tour of the pasture when, due to his advanced years, the rain that started to fall or whatever, the bull's heart gave out. This turn of events was solved rather quickly after a pointed discussion with the farmer (see BULL— $1,200 and FREEZER-$600).

The exertion of eluding the bull had left me in a weakened condition, so the rain that had been falling had the effect of giving me pneumonia and causing me to miss work ($350) and pay medical bills ($460), two more unplanned but justifiable expenses.

In any event, I recovered at length and finally managed to acquire the remaining two woodcock I required for the magazine assignment. The birds were so aquired when they flew into the windshield of my Jeep as I was returning from my Aunt Greta's funeral in Des Moines. Since I had to go to the funeral anyway, and the woodcock were extra, I only took half the cost of the Des Moines trip as a business deduction (see AUNT GRETA—$175). I did however, take the full $156.90 deduction for a new Jeep windshield as a related expense.

I now had the required three woodcock. I photographed them, even though one had been frozen nearly a year, and the other two sparkled smartly with glass splinters. I wrote the assigned story and sold it for $35, which I declared as income on my 1040 Form.

I hope this settles this matter. However, I have been assigned another story, this one about a bird called a "ruffed grouse," so you may hear from me again.

Cordially,
Steven R. Smith

The Woodcock
Gun

Think for a minute about someone, anyone, you'd like to sit down with in front of a good log fire and talk about bird hunting. Between you sits a bottle of Virginia Gentleman bourbon, Angostura bitters and an ice bucket with dogs on it. The glasses are huge, sweating and have the smell and color of October.

My man is a good friend I've never met. Yet I'm sure that where he lives right now is just fine, a freshening walk from some alder bottoms where the woodcock fly like bats at sundown—and the surrounding gentle hills are salt-and-peppered with birches and spruce trees and therein live the Lord's own pet flock of grouse.

I'd like to meet him there someday because I own his gun. Let's say I have it in safe keeping for the time being and will someday pass it on to someone else—some other woodcock nut.

It's a little English Greener, 16 gauge, 24-inch barrels side-by-side, bored half choke and improved. It has a top safety (a rarity in a Greener) and a superb selective single trigger, with just a whisper of a pistol grip and a leather covered recoil pad. The stock is, of course, Circassian. The receiver is in the grey and gently scrolled. It's just shy of 5¾ pounds—but you wouldn't think it weighed that much; it's just there, and it flies to the shoulder like a shadow. It was made in Birmingham, England, back in 1912. It cost 56 pounds, about $280, back in those old hard money days. According to the letter I got from Greener, it was sold, special order, to this friend of mine, through the long forgotten Boston Hardware Company. They never knew his name or where he really lived. How I'd like to know the man who had it made! He must have been an independent Yankee cuss. I'll bet it was the only 24-inch side-by-side in all New England. There must have been some laughs and jokes around the cider mill when he first showed it off!

I like to think I know just how he dressed. An old felt hat with the crown pushed down all around so it would make a watering cup for his dog. And for comfort's sake he'd have had his wife cut the long sleeves off his once brown hunting coat. (Wind and rain must have bleached the canvas to butternut.) I suspect he wore a necktie when he shot his birds.

In the back of his hunting buggy, drawn by some sweet-breathed old mare, would be just-turned apple cider and some bitter ale, wrapped in dampened feed sacks to keep them cool and, without a doubt, some corn meal cakes for his Gordon setter.

He would be getting on in years when he had the little Greener 16 made. I suspect the time had come to save those steep New England apple orchard hillside covers for some other day that rarely came. But you know how hard it is to pass by those crisp Fall Pippins, Northern Spies, or huge Pound Sweets. (My greying Labrador likes nothing better than to sit and chew stolen apples while I smoke my pipe—I think he would have liked old Tippy.)

My best guess is that this little Greener was born for the alder bottoms and the mythical flights of woodcock; if you like woodcock, you love the swamps. I'm sure he had one absolutely perfect bottom cover. There'll be one or two small creeks that pass near by. Not too much heavy grass because the farmer turns his dry cows out here to graze and fertilize the ground and feed the earthworms that the woodcock banquet on. And deep inside these alders is one perfect, cold clear spring. This whole cover's not too big—I'd guess a damned good 30-minute hunt at most. It must be wet, but not too wet.

Warm, but not hot. Changing air, but not windy. And being just exactly right, it hunts best by walking east since we're sure he saves it, being best, for last, and wouldn't want the setting sun shining in his eyes.

His old Gordon setter, saddled black and tan, must have really loved this bottom. A nice cool drink, soft mud on his tired feet and best of all, the lovely umber-colored smell of woodcock. Three more birds in the bag with five handloaded shells—and back to the buggy. Cider or ale, rat cheese, hard bread, fill the pipe, cluck the mare awake and down the old dirt road. The old setter listens to the creaking axle springs, snuggles in the fresh marsh hay under the seat for a little nap and home just after dark.

My Labrador, grey-chinned Tippy, looks up at me as I put the little Greener back under the hand-rail on the crooked stairs that wind behind my fireplace. How often has this gun been wiped with loving care, swung one last time, and set away in some homemade deerhorn rack to be admired?

Here's a toast to you, old friend, who made this perfect gun come true. All Good. And I promise that as long as wood-cock whistle and good dogs sleep at our feet while we sit before the fire and drink whiskey . . . you'll be remembered.

Gene Hill

The Primrose
Path

There are certain natural laws that we have all learned to live with that are as constant and valid as the fact of gravity. Laws like "if anything can possibly go wrong it will." "Nothing is impossible to the man who doesn't have to do it." "Never do today what can be put off until tomorrow." "Things are never as bad as they seem ... they're usually worse."

Now, what our language is sorely missing is some law to explain the phenomena that happen to the guy who likes to spend a little time out-of-doors. You likely know the pattern all too well. It starts in a variety of ways but buying a puppy is as common as any. Now, more than not, one of the first dogs you think of is an English setter—just because they're pretty. Then you discover as the dog is growing up that it is pointing the robins on the lawn. So you figure if the dog will point robins ... why not take the next logical step and see if it will point quail or pheasants? Unhappily for you—it does.

The next step is borrowing a neighbor's gun and buying a license to take a shot or two to see if the dog can help you pick up a nice bird or so for Sunday dinner. Then it's hunting clothes. Memberships in a local gun club to practice your wing shooting. Then it's discovered that you need at least *three* guns: one for birds, one for skeet, one for trap. Then it's either a lot of expensive trips to find better bird hunting or an expensive membership in a shooting preserve. Now your dog is in heat and you start looking for a good male so you can have just one more dog. Or vice versa.

You now have at least three guns, an enormous wardrobe of gear, memberships in various gun clubs, shooting clubs, field trial and dog clubs. And you've traded in a perfectly good family sedan for a new station wagon. You start smoking a pipe. You discover that the pleasant smell around the fire in the lodge is only part woodsmoke—the other part is bourbon. You seem to get sick a lot in the fall so you can't show up at the office. You have started to shout DOWN! HUP! OVER! at your children and barely caught yourself in time to keep from telling your wife HEEL! Your good suit is always covered with dog hair and so is the house and the car. There are teeth marks in all the chair rungs and your good leather boots. Your expensive shrubbery is a horror and none of the words a preacher uses on Sunday could describe your lawn.

But not to mind. A man can have worse habits than three guns and some bird dogs—not more expensive or time consuming—but there are worse.

Pretty soon a friend of yours will stop over and start chucking your puppy behind those silken ears and begin asking your advice. Chances are you will start to speak with forked tongue as our Indian friends used to say. You will describe the dawn smell of the meadows with a soft persuasive voice . . . speak lightly of your acquired skill with a shotgun and dwell longingly on campfires and twilights as you top his glass with a fresh dash or two. You offer him your can of Brushsmoke to fill his pipe. By now he's too far swept away into some imagined October afternoon to notice that his suit is covered with dog hair and pipe ashes have scorched little holes in his tie.

You lend him your copy of Ray Holland's *Seven Grand Gun Dogs* and Burton Spiller's *Firelight* and send him off to sail by new stars.

It's just another one of nature's immutable laws that we are all bound by. Some might say that it's "Misery loves company." But we know better. It's really more like "God doesn't count the hours man spends afield with friends," or "The thing we build that lasts longest is memory." All we ever need to do to hear the sounds of geese is listen. All we ever need to do to see the point and the flush is to close our eyes.

Gene Hill

Guns, Loads
and the Methods

No amount of advice by any book on hunting will encourage the reader of said advice to rush out and buy a brand new shotgun. Most grouse and woodcock are bagged by shooters who are using what they have on hand, and thousands of the birds fall each year to long-barreled pump-guns as well as full-choked autos. More birds are knocked down by 12-gauges than anything else, and even the .410 accounts for quite a few of the Tawny Twisters.

But for the devoted grouse and woodcock nut, there is no gun quite so suited to the flight of these upland sprites as the 20-gauge double.

Let's pretend that you and I are going, tomorrow, on your first-ever grouse and woodcock hunt. Your great Aunt Emma from Terra Haute left you, her favorite nephew, a sizable sum in her will with the instructions that it be spent only on foolishness and frivolity. You have just asked me what type of piece you should purchase for the sole purpose of downing grouse and woodcock. I, for my part, am only too happy to oblige. Freshening our glasses of bourbon, and refilling my favorite pipe, I lean back in my chair, stretch my legs as much as the setter crowding my feet allows, and gaze into the flames licking the white-ash logs in the fireplace. The wind hums a chilly autumn tune over the cabin eaves.

With the scene set, then, and the pleasant talk of guns and loads in the offing, I'd respond something like this: "Let's start off with woodcock. If you are going to be a woodcock hunter, not just an opportunistic woodcock shooter, you'll want to be armed right. That is, you'll want to have the gun that will do the most effective job, will give you the greatest pride of ownership, and will get you into action the fastest. Also, you'll want a gun that lends itself to easy pointing in the thick stuff, which automatically precludes any gun with a single sighting plane, such as a pump, auto, or over-under. Naturally, that leaves only the side-by-side double. That, of course, is what I shoot, and with good reason.

"The side-by-side, you see, down-flips a bit because there's somewhat less support for the barrels. This means that the thing can be stocked a bit higher and straighter, which allows you to really see the bird and the barrels, out of focus of course. The twin tubes also allow you to point better because they look like a highway out there against the brush. I can't prove it, but I'll bet that most champion skeet shooters would choose a side-by-side if their favorite skeet field suddenly sprouted 15 foot high alders and aspen trees. It's just too easy to lose track of the skinny barrel of an over-under or repeater in the brush, especially when the light's bad.

"Naturally, you'll want to see the bird ABOVE the barrels, so this straight stock business makes good sense. Since money is no object with you, I'd suggest that you find out your measurements and get cracking on a custom stock right off.

"Next, of course, is gauge. The 20 appears to be just right. It carries light, and the shells weigh little, but it is still ballistically efficient and will kill 'cock dead with proper pointing. No gauge will kill them dead if it's pointed wrong.

"When you're ordering this piece, specify 25- or 26-inch barrels, and make the right barrel a no choke tube—straight cylinder. With today's modern loads, straight cylinder is going to give you a really nice pattern that opens quickly and stays even and deadly out to about 25 yards, but about 21 is perfect range. Order the left barrel improved cylinder. If a 'cock jumps and you miss, he'll probably be about 5 to 7 yards farther out when you get him again, and then the improved barrel will do its job. Besides, the cylinder barrel won't shred the birds during close, early season shooting.

"While we're at it, let's make sure that your gun has automatic ejectors, but single or double triggers are your choice. Personally, it's all I can do to get the safety off and get on the bird without worrying about selecting a barrel or a trigger, so the number of triggers is up to you."

I pause long enough to light my pipe, and freshen your bourbon, adding an ice cube to mine.

"Now, a long time ago, some genius thought that shotguns should have things on them called "pistol grips," and a lot of folks swear by them, but the British have long since decided that the straight hand grip is the best, and there's good reason to agree. A straight grip just naturally throws your elbow up and makes your face stay down on the stock, so I'd order one built like that and learn to use it. Besides, no shotgun in the world looks better and sleeker than a side-by-side with straight grip.

"A slim, slightly beavertail forearm really polishes the thing off nicely, and gives something substantial for your left hand to grip. With the straight grip, you'll find that you're doing far more swinging with your left hand. Besides, a beavertail that is slim and unobtrusive is no heavier than a splinter once you factor in weight of the cocking and ejecting mechanisms, and it lets your left hand work, which speeds up the swing. With your left hand locked in, the gun comes up quick, fast, and solid, no jumping around and adjusting because you're trying to do all the work with your trigger hand.

"Naturally, not all shots at woodcock are going to be close, and as the season progresses, they'll get longer as cover gets knocked down. So, order another gun, or an extra set of barrels for your original, with everything the same except the borings. Order this set or gun improved cylinder and modified for late season work, or when you think you may be in a grouse/woodcock cover and shots will be a bit longer. I use identical guns, except for boring, only because I like having lots of guns.

"As far as loads, I'd use #9 skeet loads in the cylinder barrel, and an ounce of 8's in the left barrel of my early season gun, and I'd switch to 8's and 7½'s when I switch guns. Wide patterns mean small shot, or else the bird will slip through or be crippled. Small shot also means short range, so don't be taking any 40 yard drags at 'cock with either of those pieces. The bird deserves better than that. Of course, you'll want the gun to weigh less than six pounds for easier carrying. Fast handling is best accomplished by proper balancing, weight being secondary unless you're a weakling."

You are now enthralled with my wisdom, and edge forward in your chair to catch every nuance of my voice. I think you are now ready for some words about shooting, so I proceed.

"Down in the brush, if you wait for a good, open shot, you'll likely never have to clean your gun, because it won't get fired. You can, though, move the odds in your favor with a little bit of technique.

"Being a good brush shot doesn't mean shooting at sound—that's dangerous, stupid, and brands you a slob. Instead, learn to hear. When you hear a bird flush, the whistling wings will give you an idea of which way and how fast the mark is departing. If this is nowhere near your partner, and you think you've got a chance, throw that little double to your shoulder and turn toward the sound. Don't release the safety, and keep your head up high. Pop your eyeballs out as far as you can, and strain for a glimpse of the bird. When you're like this, you're at least 80% ready. Now, if the woodcock appears so you can see him well, drop your face to the stock, push the safety off, swing with a quick little stroke until your brain tells you that you are in front, and touch off. If you wait to mount until you actually see the bird, you'll eat sardines for supper instead of broiled woodcock on toast.

"Also, forget that nonsense about woodcock rising and leveling off and shooting at the top of their spin. I haven't seen more than a dozen birds do that in a dozen years. If the cover is somewhat open, they'll go out low and fast—fast as a grouse, and they'll dodge trees like a brokenfield runner. Dwell on 'em and you'll miss.

"If you are in thick stuff, though, they will head for daylight, so watch any holes in the canopy. When old Missy here points them, you've got some time to get set and look around. Course, as sure as you think you've got it figured out, they'll go right in the opposite direction. You'll only learn by experience.

"There's also been way too much written about being fast," I continue.

"The need to be fast is not nearly as important as the average person thinks. In fact, most of the really good brush shooters that I know are past middle age. That should tell you that it is being smooth and experienced that counts. Let's do a little arithmetic. Let's say that a really peppy woodcock flushes five yards ahead of you and flies straight away through an opening in the cover. He's traveling at—and let's not be conservative—25 miles an hour. That's, let's see what my figuring says, about 36 feet a second. That means that even after two full seconds the bird is only about 29 yards away, and that's if he's going straight away, thus putting the most distance possible between herself and the gun. Now, if your gun is mounted at the 80% position on the initial flush, and that takes maybe three quarters of a second even if you do it ver-r-ry carefully, that leaves one and a quarter seconds to locate the bird, see it clearly, get your cheek down and slap the trigger—plenty of time. Usually, about 20 yards from your position is where such a 'cock would be hit.

"If you find yourself missing a lot, don't go trading guns around like Hilly does his trap guns. Stick with one and the birds will fall. Above all, don't take any shots which may endanger your partner, your dog, or somebody in the cover you may not even be aware is present. If the bird goes out too low, let him go, there will be others or you'll get him up again.

"Birds going away over your head have to be shot by holding under; birds below your eye level going away—provided you're sure of the background—have to be held over because they are, in effect, rising. Now do you see why I told you to get a straight stocked gun and learn to shoot it? With one that shoots dead level by looking straight down the rib, you'd have to cover such a bird up to hit it. It's pretty tough to hit a bird that's covered by your barrels."

By now, you are ready to vote for me for President or offer your eldest daughter in marriage. My words and the bourbon have you in a state of euphoria, so you ask me the inevitable, "What is good woodcock shooting?" I ponder this a bit, and then answer.

"It depends on where you are. On a sunny hillside, you can stack them up like cordwood if you've a mind to do it that way or need a full limit to call it a good day. If you go down in the alders where the real sportsman hunts, then you'll do worse.

"If I had to put a number on it, I'd say that a man who can shoot 50% on woodcock, day in and day out for several seasons, can be called a crack shot. Most will shoot one out of four. By this, I mean that if a man has fired four shells and has one woodcock to show for it, he's a solid average. If he has two birds and four empties, he's allowed to crow—provided he can do it again tomorrow and the next day and the next.

"I remember one time my gunning partner, Mark Sutton, came home from a business trip in Texas and hadn't shot his gun for over a full year. He picked it up and we hit the Old Orchard cover just after first light. I'd been hunting quite a bit and shooting skeet more than my wife would like. Anyway, Sutton kills the first four birds he shoots at and I miss eight straight. Naturally, he's ecstatic because we usually shoot about the same—mediocre. The next day, he gets two birds with nine shells, and I go three for four—and this is after he had a day to limber up. You just can't tell what the birds will do, so don't try to outguess them too much. Stay loose and flexible.

"I remember once when I just got a new double I was convinced would make me whispered about in reverent terms wherever good shooters gather. I went out and folded up the first bird old Tracy pointed. Well, I was on cloud nine. Know what happened? I missed 16 shots in a row, 16 shots! Naturally, like a beginner, I traded the gun in on something more expensive. Sutton said that I could have gone one-for-17 with a hand-axe, and I couldn't have done much worse than I did. Most guys give up on 'cock guns and woodcock before they learn how to hit them. Stick with it. Skeet helps, if you use your bird gun, but the best practice is just hunting. 'Cock will give you enough shots to get good in the course of a few seasons, so the key is to stay at it.

"Now the grouse," I say matter-of-factly, "is quite a fellow. He's got eyes on the back of his head, and the ability to beat you at every turn for a couple reasons: First off, because he's so damned fast, and secondly because of where he lives. Put him in an open field and you'll probably miss few. Throw in a woodlot full of thick, thorny cover, and he's tough to see, let alone shoot.

"Also, he usually flushes at ranges that are beyond a normal woodcock flush, and so that means tighter boring. When I'm after grouse, I tote that little improved and modified double in 20-gauge you see in the rack there. I also have a tendency to use an ounce of 8's in the right barrel, and an ounce of 7½'s in the left when I'm after grouse, even when the cover thins and the birds grow longer feathers. There's a reason why I don't switch shot sizes, and I'll get to that in a minute.

"You see, early in the season, the cover is thick. Leaves are everywhere, and if you can see a bird at all, it's only for a quick glimpse. Try to remember to shoot by using that 80% technique I was describing earlier and you'll get some shots. Also, if everything looks right on your swing, don't hold off just because the bird cuts behind some leaves or a tree. Shoot anyway, and then get over there in a hurry with the dog. I always assume I've hit every such shot and look accordingly. I pick up a few birds each year that way.

"Does grouse shooting ever get easier?" you ask. "Well, it never gets easy, but as the season progresses, the cover gets knocked down and leaves fall, and things are a little more even. Now, you can see the bird as it gets off the ground if you've got your eyes focused out in front and not on your feet.

"Now, you can see the bird for a full two seconds, some-times, and you've got more time. But don't forget, he's carry-ing the mail, so you can't dawdle. By the same token, his noisy flush makes you think he's moving with the speed of light when actually he's in range longer than you'd think. At this time and really any time, he's going to flush toward thicker cover, unlike the woodcock which'll flush toward openings quite often. Most birds I kill at this time of year are taken at about 25 yards—not too far at all. His noise makes him easy to locate and use the brush-shooting method I described earlier.

"In the late season, and if snow has fallen, things can get even easier. At this time of the year, the birds are isolated to-gether because of lack of cover and low food supplies into what's available. Furthermore, they don't want to use any ex-cess energy, so they sit tighter. Last year I stood in one spot and counted six grouse coming out of the same blowdown in December. At such times, shots are closer, and even though the birds have thicker feathers, as I said earlier, since the shots are closer, it balances out. That's why I don't switch loads at all through the grouse season.

"One nice thing to consider. By the time the woodcock have left for the year, the cover is down well enough to hunt grouse effectively. That's why I switch guns about the third week of October or so. Once the leaves are down, any shot I get will need the improved/modified borings, whether it's a grouse or a late migrating woodcock.

"To tell you the truth, I like to be out hunting them in the snow anyway. The tracks they leave are a good indication of where the birds are concentrated, even though you'd go crazy trying to follow those tracks. Besides, winter is a nice time to be out. Most states don't have a late grouse season, but some do and it has not hurt the population one bit.

"But if I had to pick a month to hunt, it'd be from mid-October to mid-November when the cover is down but the weather's nice. For me, by far the best days to hunt are the still, sunny days when I can catch the birds on sloping hillsides facing the sun. They're dusting or just resting, and such days are great for a dog too, if there's no wind and the morning dew is hanging on for better scenting.

"Second best days to be out is when there's a light drizzle or rain. The scenting for the dog is perfect, but the birds hang out in thick stuff like alder swales and dogwood patches. Shooting is tough, and it's wet, but you get a lot of good points. The birds hold better too, seeming to hate to get wet flying or something.

"Snowy days are the same, but scenting is less good if it's snowing heavily. Wind is real bugaboo. High wind puts the birds on edge, and they'll flush wild if they hear you coming. If you work into the wind, the dog gets a lot of stray scent and can't pinpoint the bird well. If you hunt with the wind behind you—which you shouldn't be doing—the birds flush wild and the wind cleanses the cover of scent before you get to where he was. Try putting a cigar in the grass on a windy day and watch what happens to the smoke. Scent's the same way, and the dog has a hell of a time locating the bird. On top of all that, usually you can't even hear the bird flush. A lot of people don't realize that a grouse can fly as silently as an owl if he wants to, and on windy days the sound of the wind in the trees covers up his sound perfectly. You've really got to see a bird on windy days to get a shot because locating them just by sound is out.

"Another thing to consider is rainfall and how dry the ground is. In wet years, the birds are scattered throughout good cover. In dry years, the birds are concentrated in the cover that's growing along streambeds or lakeshores. If you have been finding birds here in dry years, keep after them there even when the rains come and end the drought. It takes a few weeks for them to realize it's okay to go back to their original haunts after spending the summer near water."

At this point, you reach for the bourbon again and start asking more about shooting.

"What can I reasonably expect to shoot as an average when I'm grouse hunting," you say. "About the same as woodcock?"

"Not hardly. If I had to put a figure on it, I'd say that one bird for every four shells was damned good. Probably one out of six is acceptable, but until you get the hang of it, one out of 10 or 12 is okay. I know fellows who claim they average 50%, but they never seem to do it when I'm along. Of course, a good dog helps out, especially by finding downed birds. Losing a grouse is a terrible experience, so I'm going to give you some tips on how to beat the odds by knowing what to look for as the bird is hit.

"If a bird starts cartwheeling as he's hit, you can bet your fanny that he's got a broken wing. Get the dog over there as soon as you can, because there's probably nothing wrong with his legs and he'll use 'em.

"If you see the bird fluff his feathers out as you shoot, but otherwise keep on flying, he's been hit in the body by a pellet or two and he'll likely die hidden unless you get to him fast. A bird that sets his wings will be found dead, but they don't give off much scent, so get there fast and keep your eye on the spot where you figure he went down. Last year I let off both barrels at a grouse and on the second shot, he started gliding. Sure enough, I found him in a patch of wintergreen berries in the open, his wings spread. They're shot in the vitals when they do that.

"You'll also hear a lot about grouse that tower, or fly straight up after being shot at. I've only seen it once, but when they come down, they're dead, almost always head shot. They won't come down where they went up, so get ready to run when this happens—the dog won't be much help because the bird will be airwashed when he gets down, and being dead he doesn't give off scent like a live bird does.

"If a grouse drops a leg, he may either be dead when you find him, or he may still be able to fly, but he can't run. Again, get the dog over to make the retrieve. I used to think all birds that drop a leg would be found dead, but I got fooled last season by one that took off again with that leg hanging. We got him, but I was mighty surprised.

"If the bird claps his wings to his sides and tucks his feathers in, he's also body shot, and likely to run. A bird that goes totally limp in the air and flops his head back is dead right there, and you can pick him up at your leisure. Sometimes, these birds will be head shot also and will lay in the grass and beat their wings until you locate them, stone dead. The first grouse I ever shot did that. He had one shot in the head, that was all, but he was stone dead.

"When you work a cover, try to keep your feet on the ground, especially when good cover is coming up. The birds will jump when you stop and then start up again. Before I hunted with dogs much, I used to get my share of shots by walking up to a tangle, stopping and waiting for a minute, and then shuffling my feet in the leaves. The birds had figured I'd spotted them, and took off. By the same token, if you think that a bird may be in a certain spot but you can't see well enough to shoot there, keep walking steadily and loudly until you are where you want to be. Grouse are afraid of you if they don't know where you are. If you can approach a patch of cover from an angle so you aren't walking directly at the birds, they'll figure you aren't coming after them and sit tight. When you get close and stop, they panic and take off.

"I like to carry the gun, when walking, with the barrels pointed straight up, and the butt resting on my hip. When mounting, the forearm drops straight down into my left hand when the stock comes up to my shoulder. I can go either way with it, and I don't have to swing back across my body when the gun is held this way like I would if the piece were carried in the "port arms" position you hear so much about. Also, any accidental discharge will go straight up, not at an angle through the cover. When I walk in on a point, I keep the muzzles high, but raise the stock until it is under my right shoulder, against the ribs. The muzzles are at eye level. This way, I've got a clear field of fire no matter which way the bird goes. I just finish the mount, swing fast, and shoot.

"The right type of hat, oddly enough, can affect your shooting. Walk over there and take that little 20 out of the rack." You do as I ask, hefting it carefully, keeping your fingers from the metal surfaces.

"Now, put on that hat right there that my kids got me for

fishing, the one that looks like a baseball cap. That's it, put it on so it feels comfortable. Now, throw that gun to your shoulder and point at something on the far wall. Tell me what you see."

"I see nothing but the bill of the cap," you answer.

"Exactly my point," I remark. "In order to see the mark, you've got to raise your head a bit, subconsciously lifting the hat's brim out of the way. When you do that, you raise your face from the stock, the barrels come up, and presto! You're now shooting high. You miss and you don't know why. Now, try that one with the orange hatband and the narrow brim that goes all the way around. Do the same thing. What do you see?"

"I see the mark I'm pointing at, and the brim is out of the way," you remark.

"Right, and that hat will save your scalp from the brush, keep the hair and sweat out of your eyes, and even channel the rain off your head and away from your neck, all the things a shooter's hat should do."

By now, the fire has burned down to just a few intermittent flickers of light, and our eyes are drooping. I glance at my watch, which says 11:10 P.M.

"Well, let's tune in the weather report," I say. The report calls for clear skies and winds from the northwest all night, not strong, but steady.

"Hmmm," I muse, "that means the woodcock will be moving in the Little Cedar River covers. I've got three dandies over there. Looks like a good morning's shoot."

You don't hear me, though. My monologue and the Wild Turkey have taken effect, and you are far away in some dreamy cover, where the birds are all straightaways and you come home with the left barrel still clean and a pair of grouse and a limit of five 'cock tucked in your game bag.

Of course, the preceding events were fictitious, but, hopefully, a lot can be learned from them. There are a few other points, though, which should be stressed whenever guns for woodcock are discussed. The number one priority is the patterning of these guns. I'm not going to go into great detail about patterning a shotgun. That has been done far better in other, more technical works.

However, there is one bit of advice I'd like to pass on. Do your pattern testing at 40 yards to get the percentages only if you can't live without knowing. But don't forget the closer range patterning. You'll take a lot more shots at 10 yards than you ever will at 30, so get a look at your patterns at 10, 15, 20, 25, and 30 yards to see if everything looks nice and even. If not, switch shot size, brands, or take the gun to a good choke specialist and have him see what he can do.

To show what ranges woodcock are shot, I killed birds taken with the first barrel at an average distance of a bit over 13 yards for each of the last five years I've kept records. If I used the left barrel, the average range was slightly over 19 yards, showing that in the woodcock covers, almost any choke is too much. On grouse, I average 22 yards right barrel, and 28 yards left—still good close range.

If I had to use a repeater, or swore I couldn't shoot a double, I'd buy a light automatic in 20-gauge and I'd take a hacksaw to the barrel, or—better yet—have a gunsmith do it, and I'd have a straight cylinder piece. This is the ticket for woodcock—lots of even pattern.

There are some who prefer the 12-gauge gun for grouse and woodcock because of "wider pattern." A little work at the pattern board will show this to be false. A 20, 28, or even a .410 bored the same way will throw a pattern the same size. The difference, then, is density. The 12-gauge will throw a denser pattern, and therefore allow fewer birds to slip through the pattern at marginal ranges.

However, the ranges themselves are short and therefore this is not usually a problem. A bigger consideration is the weight and handling characteristics of the gun itself. A 20, on the average, handles faster than a 12 and is efficient enough to handle the brush-shooting requirements.

Now, a light-weight 12 will do a good job. In fact, a light, cylinder-bored repeater is absolute blue murder on woodcock, and an improved-cylinder barrel will be great on grouse. A 12-gauge bored improved-cylinder and cylinder would be a fine all-around gun for both grouse and woodcock. When you go to the 20, however, the combination is fine for 'cock, but when grouse are the main target, you need at least one barrel bored modified to densify the pattern. One other factor is the tendency for an ounce-and-an-eighth of shot from a 12 to shred a woodcock at close range. Some authorities suggest shooting the close birds with the edge of the pattern. I wish I could. I usually miss them when trying to use the center of the pellet spread, let alone the edge. An ounce of shot from a 12, however, will destroy no more birds than the 20, loaded with an ounce of shot.

Many shooters are going to the 28-gauge. Many fine, imported doubles can be had in this gauge, as well as a few domestic jobs. Remington makes a 28-gauge in both lightweight pump and autoloader configuration. This gun is very efficient, ballistically, and in a double is quite fast. However, it may be best for woodcock alone, and not for grouse, except in the hands of a real expert.

A good part of the speed of a piece has to do with the balance of the gun. A pump or auto can be balanced like a double, but this usually entails adding weight to the stock to balance the barrel. Naturally, this makes the thing a little heavier to carry.

The lightweight gun fetish, however, shouldn't get out of hand, especially with a grouse gun. A too light gun makes for jerky swings and is even slower because it comes up to the shoulder pretty quickly, but then it bounces around out there on the barrel end. After you've corrected and corrected again, the bird may be gone. A little more weight brings it up right and solid. This difference may be only the location of a few ounces, say the difference between a slim beavertail forearm and a splinter or sliver forearm. I prefer the slim beavertail for hard-flying grouse because of this factor. One gun of mine has both types, made up for me by Gunsmith Dick Williams, and I can't shoot the splinter. With a straight grip, I need something tangible for my left, or forearm hand, because it does so much guiding of the swing. The beavertail does this better than the splinter.

When I started off grouse and woodcock hunting, I had no old time expert shooter to help me along. I had to arrive at my choice of armament from experience. I shot single-barrels, pumps, autos, and doubles. I used 12's, 20's, 16's, and even a .410. Therefore, my experience has been that the 20-gauge double, for me at least, is the optimum piece with which to take grouse and woodcock in the brush.

Steve Smith

Gun Fit

Many fine articles have been written and are available for the grouse and woodcock shooter on the topic of gun fit. However, in no area of shooting is gun fit so important as it is in the brush. In a duck blind, the shooter usually has time to get his cheek down, and fast shooting is usually not required on flushing ringnecks, but on grouse and woodcock, he who hesitates eats spam.

Therefore, the gun should fit according to the shooter's personal measurements. I prefer a simple approach to gun fit. If you hit your nose with your thumb when you shoot, the stock is too short. If it catches in your clothing, it's too long—unless you aren't mounting it properly and getting sloppy.

If you throw up a double and can see only the end bead, it is stocked too low at the comb. However, with single sighting plane guns, such as pumps, autos or the over/under, this is all you SHOULD see. The double allows you to see more barrel and the bird above it, as discussed earlier. However, many more men are taking the tack that all guns should be stocked high so that they can shoot up at the bird and can thus see it better. This keeps the cheek down on the stock better.

A too-low stock recoils too much, and a gunsmith can inlet wood into the comb to raise the point of impact. He can sand down a comb that's too high to lower impact. Adding a rib to a repeater will lower impact without touching the stock, and even a big bead on the end will cause the shooter to subconsciously hold lower on the mark.

One area that is often overlooked is pitch, the angle of the stock where it's cut off at the butt. Pitch up will let the stock slip up during the mounting and between shots at a double.

The best way I know of determining fit is to go to a patterning range and shoot patterns at the board as fast as you can mount and fire. By taking note of deviations of impact, you can make the proper adjustments. For example, if 10 shots at the sheets tell you that you are high, take some wood off the comb or add down-pitch by inserting some spacers under the screw holding the top of the butt plate in place. Try this first before hacking on your stock.

Once you've got the proper fit, practice with the gun. I like to shoot skeet with my bird guns, and good pre-season practice can be had by going to the gun club when things are slow and having the trap boy pull targets for you while you stand directly behind the traphouse. The boy will soon figure out that it's fun to make you miss, so he may throw two in a row quickly, hesitate to give you time to reload, and nail you again. The unexpected angle of birds from the traphouse and their method and angle of departure is much like birds going out from under a dog's point.

Another way is with hand-thrown clay targets in the brush. One spot I use is an old forest road near a local dump. My partner throws the targets down the road, and I stand off in the brush and swing with them. This allows brush shooting practice without breaking the clays on limbs and trees.

Shooting pest birds around a farmer's barn is fine too, if you can find such a place. Pigeons, starlings and sparrows offer sporting targets. The main thing to remember is that the more you practice on a variety of targets with your grouse and woodcock gun, the more familiar you'll become with it, and the better you'll shoot.

Steve Smith

Shooting Styles
and Slumps

There are situations when no amount of coaching will help you score, but in general, there are a few tips about shooting style that can be passed on.

The really good brush-shooter is the man who finds the bird quickly and has the gun 80% mounted and pointed as described earlier before he even sees the bird. Then, he has to make a quick decision about which style of swing to use. After awhile, the decision comes naturally. There are some basic kinds of swings that can help you score. FAST SWING—This first method is most often used. It consists of starting behind the bird, passing through it, and firing when the amount of daylight desired appears. For those with slow reflexes, firing as the barrel comes even with the bird will do the trick.

This type of swing is the most fool-proof, but takes practice and has to be accomplished quickly. Done perfectly, the fast swing is so fast that it looks like a snap-shot. SPOT SHOOTING—Shooting to spots means simply shooting with the barrels stationary. A true straightaway, or one in which the bird is not relatively rising or dropping from eye level is where this is used. A variation of this is to shoot at the spot that seems to be out there, ahead of the bird and moving with it. This "moving spot" is the point you will have to hold to kill the bird, and the swing is accomplished while mounting. In this type of spot shooting, the shooter pivots with the bird, and swings the gun with the mark as he mounts. By the time the gun is at the cheek, it is already pointing ahead of the bird at the moving spot, and he fires. The momentum of the mounting swing keeps the barrels moving, and precludes a miss—usually. This combination of the fast swing and spot shooting is especially helpful when there is no time to dawdle.

Most good grouse and 'cock shots have apoplexy when a bird flushes in the open. The reason is because they will generally miss this bird because they take too much time, and alter their fast, brush-shooting swings. I hate this type of shot, but a duck hunter I shoot with occasionally does great on birds in the open—when they can be found there or flush across an opening in cover. He is used to lots of time and lots of sky. He suggests the slowed-down version of the fast swing, and I'll have to try this deliberate method sometime—if I don't panic and let off both barrels at the first sound of wings.

Eventually, the shooter will become fairly proficient and down his share of birds, and that's when the slumps start. A slump is a series of unexplained misses from a gun that has always given good service in the past. Maybe the shooter has outgrown the fit. I once shot lousy at the beginning of a season until I realized that I'd gained about 15 pounds, mostly in my chubby little cheeks. This extra pad of flesh negated my gun fit, and made me shoot high. Losing the weight made the gun fit again.

Sometimes a bad string of flushes can hurt your average. When the birds come out unexpectedly, all of them at hard angles, then you can really start talking to yourself. When this happens, I start picking my shots.

Most shooters look down on picking your shots as being unsporting and a false attempt at keeping the old average up. Maybe. But, picking shots, especially at woodcock, has a lot going for it.

First, it can raise your average and end a slump, giving you confidence to try the toughies again. Secondly, it results in fewer crippled birds because you just refuse the marginal targets and take the sure ones. You also shred fewer birds because you pass up the ultra-close bird or wait until he gets out a bit before firing.

Since you shoot less this way, you disturb a cover less, and therefore alarm fewer birds. Besides, you can build a good streak. Once, during a really bad slump, I started picking my shots and I did pretty well. Sutton hit a slump a bit later in the year, and I suggested shot picking. He tried it, and when hunting a cover, a single crisp crack marked a downed bird from his side of the cover.

In case you can't pick your shots or want to shoot at everything, just take a limited number of shells with you into a cover or load only one barrel or use only one shell. This really makes you bear down.

The opening day of grouse and woodcock season last year, I allowed myself only five shells for the day. My partner and I hit the first cover of the day and started hunting. Neil missed about a half dozen shots and I hadn't fired yet because I was picking the shots. Finally, things fell into place and I took four birds, all woodcock, with four shells in a bit over an hour. Fewer shots in a woodcock cover will also mean better dog work because woodcock will not hold well on successive flushes after they've been fired at. Shooting and missing at the same bird twice usually puts him some place where he'll flush wild by the third time. By holding off, you'll get better shooting.

By skipping marginal targets, you'll shoot better, use less ammo, shred and wound fewer birds, and disturb the cover less. All good reasons to pick your shots, at least on woodcock.

On grouse, a shot-picker may wait until he can collect his pension before he gets a decent poke. I suggest shooting at the birds as they come, provided they are in range, and hoping for the best. Ignore the brush and swing like mad. If the misses string out, usually the hits will too, eventually, and you'll be back on an even keel.

Steve Smith

Shooting the Side-by-Sides

The side-by-side question has been given new life by the relatively modest cost and high quality of some of the recent imports, like the Ithaca series and the fine Browning.

Long the traditional "gentleman's gun," the double barrel up until a short time ago was available mainly through the used-gun market. The British Webley & Scott, Winchester Model 21s, Parkers, L.C. Smiths and various long-lost American makes of fine quality—Fox, Baker, Ithaca—to remind you of the more famous makes to be had at relatively reasonable cost.

However, many shooters, used to the single sighting plane of over-and-unders, pumps and autos, often have trouble shooting the doubles as well.

But first off, if you think the wide plane of the double is bothersome, remember some names like Annie Oakley, Captain Bogardus, countless legendary British field shots who in a single season would (and still do) take thousands of difficult driven birds with very, very few misses. The point is that you can shoot what you get used to if you have proper gun fit and basically good shooting form.

The gunner who has been used to single sighting planes starts out making a major mistake in shooting a double: he makes himself too conscious of the barrel configuration. The first-rate field shot *focuses on the game—not the gun!*

Competition shooters like Billy Perdue, a long-time All-

American, shoot the toughest game of all—boxed live pigeons—with an exposed hammer side-by-side Purdey. Rudy Etchen also carries a side-by-side to the pigeon ring—and leaves with lots more than carfare in his pocket. If you attend a European pigeon shoot, where many thousands of dollars are on the line, you'll find the gun rack full of side-by-side doubles.

Why? It isn't just tradition by a long 45-yard shot. It's the reliability of the action; it's the smooth fluid feel of a well-balanced gun and the extreme quickness with which they can be pointed.

(Speaking of tradition, it does die hard in some circles. Many Purdey over-and-unders have the triggers marked Left and Right . . .)

True, you don't see the side-by-sides in any number on today's trap and skeet fields, although John Sternburger set many trap doubles records using a Winchester Model 21. But I'd like to see a Ricky Pope try one at skeet or a Dan Bonillas shoot one at trap. I don't think their scores would suffer much.

For the field gunner, the side-by-side has much to recommend it. For one thing, the balance makes it less tiring to carry—and I think they are faster pointing and quicker moving. In the confines of a duckblind, the opening of a double requires about half the room of that of an over-and-under. Much is made of the fact in Britain that a double (or over-and-under) is safer because it can be carried visibly open. (I believe the same can be said of autos and pumps, but I just remark on one more facet of their prejudice toward twin-barreled guns).

Overall gun lengths tend to be shorter in side-by-sides than in other guns, contributing to their lighter weight and more comfortable balance.

And, not last or least, it has to be unchallengeable that the aesthetics of a well-made double gun is the undeniable epitome of grace—of form following function.

Another problem that's mostly mental is the fact that most side-by-sides have double triggers. This should not require much adjustment, especially if the stock is "straight hand"—no pistol grip.

If there is any single serious drawback to shooting a side-by-side it probably lies in the area of stock fit. Most of the vintage doubles were made with a great deal of drop at heel to accommodate the head-up, "looking over the barrels" style of shooting that was prevalent at the time. I know several fine shots who still shoot this way, but it is difficult to get used to, once you've enjoyed a straighter stock configuration.

You might find, especially if you're a fast-pointing gunner, the side-by-side can get away from you a bit—and you'll overlead some of the quick crossing shots, especially with the light short-barreled, smaller gauges. You'll have to school yourself to remember that light guns make you swing way out in front, then, realizing that, you stop and either shoot or start all over. None of this works, as you know.

The classic British method of gunning in the field is still about the best: The bird is followed with the eyes, the hands swing the gun—but it is *not* mounted until the instant you are ready to shoot. At that time, the hands and eyes and gun have established the flight pattern, judged the speed and the "forward allowance"—so the second the gun is properly on the shoulder is the time to fire—no second thoughts, no more conscious swinging. It sounds too simple—but with just a little faith and practice you'll find that it works.

There are, of course, doubles that don't shoot where they should—chokes that have been tampered with, dented or bent barrels that can often go unnoticed for a long time. But barring any physical impediment, the complaint of not being able to field shoot a side-by-side has to rest with the gunner—not the gun.

If you're considering breaking out an older double that you've had for a while, or one that you've picked up—by all means have a good gunsmith look it over. Many of the old guns, especially the British ones, are short chambered and not safe or comfortable with our 2¾-inch shells. The 16s, especially, are very likely to be short chambered—even the American ones. It is very important that you make doubly sure that the safety is functioning and that the triggers are properly adjusted for the right weight of pull.

Gene Hill

The Best Gunning Companions

She wasn't very big as Brittany spaniels go, maybe 25 pounds and 15 inches at the shoulder. She was always painfully thin during bird season, regardless of the huge amounts of prime feed she got.

She had an uncanny knack of knowing when autumn had rolled around. Maybe she smelled the old gunning clothes, or the nip in the air told her that her time of year had come, but somehow she knew.

Tracy didn't belong to me in the common sense. She was owned by my shooting partner and boyhood chum, Mark Sutton, and there was never any doubt that she was a one-man dog, and I wasn't the man. Oh, I'm sure that she loved me as I loved her, but it was different. When I showed up at the farm it was hunting season, and she loved me because I was part of the hunting.

When bird hunting—grouse and woodcock—she was one of the pointing breeds that could circle ahead of a running grouse and nail him down with a solid point. She knew by experience just how close to get to a grouse or woodcock before it would flush, and she bumped very few birds.

If she had pointed, and the bird had walked off a bit to one side, she'd give a little twist of her head toward the bird while looking at me, as if to say "The bird's over here, boss!" Whatever that talent was, I enjoyed it.

We never really laid them low, Mark and I, because lay-ing them low was never our intent. Good dog work, a chance to be outside in the autumn, and enough birds for a Sunday dinner were our aims. Tracy never could understand that, and expected us to shoot at every bird she pointed. When we didn't, she'd get thoroughly exasperated with us.

She also couldn't tolerate missing, something that Mark and I did with disgusting frequency. Once, after a particularly futile attempt at collecting grouse, she forsook her accustomed position between us in my car and curled up in the back seat. She didn't sleep, but wouldn't look at us even when coaxed, and did a lot of heavy sighing.

Her last season, at age five, was her best. The weather was flawless every Saturday of the season. We hunted a lot that year, shot fairly well, and her work on pointed birds was superb.

I'll never forget that painful phone call from Mark, his voice choked and strangely subdued. Seems that the vets couldn't cope with a strange virus that wracked her thin frame. The end was quick. She'd died in her sleep, and was buried with her bell in the alder thickets she loved so much.

The thrill is somewhat gone out of autumn. There have been other dogs—better in many ways than Tracy ever was, but it's not the same, and may never be. The colors of the autumn maple are a little less brilliant, and the tinkling of a bird dog's bell in the alders doesn't ring as sweetly.

The foregoing seems to epitomize what a grouse and woodcock hunter's best friend means to him. In all sports involving birds and shotguns, the dog plays an important part. But, in this hunting, the search for true art reaches its zenith.

Let me say first, that the perfect grouse dog has never been born, at least I haven't seen it. That rather rash statement comes from years of experience in watching pretty good grousers in action, and talking to bird dog men from every part of the grouse's range.

By this I don't mean to look down upon the multitudes of canines that do a beautiful job in the autumn uplands, and bring a misty tear of joy to their owner's eye. Instead, it is a statement of fact as I see it.

If the perfect dog is nonexistent, good ones are as nearly rare as the legendary bicuspids on a chicken. They seem, unfortunately, to be getting rarer. Where, in the early part of this century a small town in good grouse country could boast of a dozen pretty fair grouse dogs, a large city or even a decent sized hamlet in excellent grouse range cannot. In the city where I live and toil, I know of only two dogs that I would call good. There may be others, but I haven't seen them, and I've seen quite a few.

The reason why so few good grousers exist today seems to be multifold. Naturally, shorter shooting seasons and shorter bag limits certainly inhibit the hours that can be spent afield hunting, and we all know it takes grouse to make a good grouse dog.

Secondly, the hubbub of modern life finds the grouse man taking his sport in snatches of a day here and an afternoon there rather than the week or two excursions by train that marked the pre-World War II days. Modern pressures have taken the man out of the field more and more. In my home state of Michigan, the average grouse hunter spent a little over seven days afield in a three-month season—September 15 to November 15, and all of the month of December. Where seasons are shorter, days afield are probably correspondingly fewer.

Besides this, there is what might be called the "papers fetish." In this mild form of mania, the purchaser of a grouse dog cares not for the dog's hunting ancestry, but only cares if the animal is registered and has papers to prove it. The last registered dog I hunted with was a flushing animal with the field manners of a Yorkshire hog, but—by God—she had papers.

Related closely with this is the feeling that any well-marked dog of the sporting breeds can turn a potential profit if bred, which has caused the overall talent pool of many breeds to become watered down. In the old days, a non-talented mutt was, well, taken out of the breeding population, so to speak. Today, the non-talented dog is sold to some unsuspecting, non-hunting buyer who in turn breeds the thing and sells these as hunting dogs, knowing no better. The last dog I looked at was a well-marked setter, small of frame and eager to please. When I inquired about her blood lines, the seller assured me she had those all important papers. When I inquired further about her hunting heritage, I was told her bitch's mother was really great shakes as a hunter. In other words, this fine looking animal that jumped on my trouser legs and begged for attention had only one proven hunter among her last eight closest relatives. I passed up the sale.

The best way I know of to get a good grouse dog, be it English setter, pointer, Brittany, shorthair or even a flushing dog such as a springer, is to watch the parents hunt. If the sire and the dam will hunt, the pups will hunt, most likely, and won't be from show-dog or home-pet stock.

The feelings of the owner himself can also affect the end result of his dog-training attempts. The owner must analyze his own attitude toward birds and dogs to see if he isn't backsliding a bit.

For example, there are two types of dog men: those who seek birds and want the dog to aid in that end, or those who like good dog work, and the birds present them with the opportunity. The former type is likely to overlook all kinds of bad habits in a dog in his pursuit of game. Habits such as breaking to wing or shot, blinking, hardmouth, or even failing to always obey the whistle or hand signals. In his quest for birds, the man thinks of the dog as another four feet in the woods to help him bag his limit of birds, and we'll just overlook the bad habits.

The latter type of gent goes the other way. He only shoots at birds that the dog has pointed, and wants the animal to react as a mere extension of his own thoughts. This man's dogs must always be quartering, must always turn outward on the turns, and must follow hand signals impeccably. In addition, the dog has to sit to deliver the bird to hand, must drop it only on the signal "give," and must honor another dog's point always.

To me, it seems there has got to be a happy medium. I've

hunted a great deal with both types of shooters, and have seen dogs that ran from undisciplined delinquents to browbeaten masses of shivering canine protoplasm.

I guess, the man has to make up his mind what he wants from a dog. Does he want a companion who is fun to be with? Does he want a pal who can share his noon-time sandwich, help him cry about his lousy shooting, and maybe not mind suggesting that the cover should be worked into the wind instead of with it? If so, then the man must make sacrifices, look the other way, and realize that dogs are human too—subject to mistakes.

I guess I am more the shooter type rather than the dog man. If I get some decent dog work, make a few hits, and see the sun shine on the autumn leaves, I'm happy. To this end, I like a dog that will show me birds, even if I have to put up with a little bird bumping. I'll shoot at a bird the dog hasn't flushed, but that I moved myself, although I won't shoot at a bird the dog bumped—that's carrying things too far. In short, I like a self-thinker who can reason things out for himself, and loves doing it.

If a grouse hunter pays a trainer to do his dog work for him, he usually expects a crack job, even though it's difficult or impossible to find a handler who can guarantee work on grouse. Usually, some other bird is substituted, like game-farm quail. I understand this, and so should anyone who sends the Pooch to a professional.

However, the man who trains the dog himself usually is content with something less, because he did it. I have a shelf in my den that I built myself. Things sometimes roll off it onto the floor, and the stain didn't take just right in some spots, but I like it. If I'd hired a cabinetmaker to do that job, I'd kick a fit that could be heard clear to Nome, Alaska if his shelf came out like mine.

So the choice is up to you. Pick you breed, pick your approach to dog training, get a good book on the subject, and go at it.

A word, here, about the flushing breeds and the pointing dogs. I much prefer the pointing breeds because I like the feeling of my heart shaking hands with my tonsils when that bell stops in the grouse covers. In addition, woodcock, as we'll see in a minute, is a bird absolutely made for a pointing dog, and I hunt both.

But, a good flusher can show you birds that a pointer may have missed. Here, we come to the argument of the close-working dog vs. the "big goer." With today's grouse covers, small and intimate and surrounded by unproductive land, I think that a close-working dog is the ticket. Others may disagree, but I like to see a dog work, not take off like a racehorse through the cover. This has nothing to do with the big-going dog flushing birds wild, although many do. Instead, it has to do with the intimacy of the cover/man/dog/bird relationship. I like to get down in there and pop brush with the dog, not let a wide-ranging dog let me do my hunting by proxy. Furthermore, I think that a close-working animal—and I don't mean underfoot, but at least in sight or usually in sight—adds to the hunt because I can watch him work out scent and do his stuff.

Naturally, it takes years to build a good grouse dog, even with a lot of work. The average good grouser hits his prime at about age three or four, and is productive well into the double digit years. What is lost in stamina and sense of smell is made up in experience, much like the human companion.

A good grouse dog knows how to hook around and pin a running bird, works the cover so that the wind will be a help, not a hindrance. He knows how to back point so that at least one animal is visible to the shooter when he goes in to flush. He delivers the bird to hand, somewhat, and takes off again to look for more, happily, and above all, he's ready to go the next day and every day.

There are books that can tell how to cure specific faults that a dog develops, faults they've usually been given by a tyro trainer/owner. There are a few faults, though, that nobody can really train out of a dog. I used to hunt with a young pointer that couldn't start a hunt unless she had run full tilt up and down a forest road. No amount of coaxing would make her hunt right out of the car. She seemed to sense that she had to work off a little enthusiasm before she went at it in earnest.

Another wouldn't go into patches of blackberry or some other thorny cover without smoothing her coat out thoroughly, as if checking out her armor before battle. How do you correct faults like this, if indeed they are faults?

Still a third dog demanded—and got—half a bologna sandwich each morning before she'd start hunting. Nothing else would work, not even raw hamburger. It had to be bologna with lots of mustard, and she preferred white bread, thank you. No sandwich—no hunt.

I think if all hunters would examine themselves a bit, they wouldn't be so tough on the dog. What type of creature would spend literally thousands of dollars on grouse hunting over a lifetime for so precious few pounds of meat? Certainly not a totally sane or rational one. Can we in good conscience expect more of our four-footed companions?

Although it can be said of woodcock hunting, to a greater extent in grouse hunting, the shooter can help both himself and the dog by observing some manners of conduct. Observing these will give him many more shots at woodcock, and will give him some at grouse where he may get none by ignoring them.

First of all, try to keep talking down to an absolute minimum. Signal a point with a low whistle, for example, instead of screaming "point." A woodcock may hold through this, but a grouse usually won't, and in most covers you have no way of knowing for sure which the dog has pinned.

Secondly, get to the point as quickly as possible. With woodcock, you may wish to alternate flushes, but with grouse it makes good sense to get to the point as quickly as you can, which means the closer man does the flushing. Alternating flushes on grouse gives the bird a chance to slip away or run and flush behind some screening cover and nobody gets a shot.

In addition, taking the shots as they come, and the points that are closest to you as they come, encourages the shooter to get down in there with the dog and help out. A shooter who knows the next grouse point is his may have a tendency to hunt the easier cover, knowing he's going to be the next one to shoot, so why beat the brush so hard?

When approaching the dog, approach from a side where the dog can see you, and do so quickly and steadily. You aren't going to be able to sneak up on the bird, so why try? Instead, move in steadily and be ready.

By being ready, the position for the shot has to be considered. I like to carry the gun tucked up under my right armpit, muzzles pointed forward. This way I can go any way the bird does—usually.

If a good grouse dog, like an honest man, is hard to find, this is not so when woodcock are the game under consideration. The reason, I am sad to say, is that almost any mediocre mutt can do a passable job of handling woodcock, and a fairly decent dog looks like a worldbeater on 'cock.

By now, the dog fanciers in the crowd, of which there are many reading this, are ready to hang my miserable carcass to rot in the autumn sunlight. But, it's true: A dog that can't hold running ringnecks, has a hard time pinning down an old rooster grouse, and gives up on quail pattering through the palmettos, can give his master reason to rejoice when woodcock are the quarry.

I wish I had a nickel for every time I've heard some citizen squawk that Old Belle was the world's greatest woodcock finder, as witnessed by the way that she pins down those birds so that there's no way they can walk away from her point. If Old Belle could handle grouse that way, or nailed down pheasants in a similar manner, I'd pay homage to this animal in song and verse. With woodcock, I remain unimpressed.

The truth of the matter is that the woodcock just doesn't run from under a point like some birds do. The birds' protective coloration is so perfect, that years of evolution have demanded that the birds defend themselves by freezing tight and waiting for the four-footed intruder to pass. This, of course, is exactly what the dog and hunter are after, and the dog seems to handle the birds beautifully.

This is not to say that woodcock will not flush prematurely, or that they can't be bumped by an incautious canine, it just means that any dog that can't find and pin 80% of the birds he should come in contact with ought to be ground up and fed to the pigeons in the park. If I could smell them, I could point 80% of the birds in a cover, so well do they hold.

Another trait long worshipped by woodcock hunters is the "working close" ethic so admired by grouse and brush-country quail shooters. Let's take an example.

About three years ago, I did a fair amount of woodcock hunting with a man who used a Lab to find his birds. Old Tar would flush every bird right up in front of the gun, and his master would break into what resembled epic poetry every time the dog made a find. The man especially admired, and pointed out, how the dog "worked close" so the birds didn't flush wild.

Well, work close he did. In fact, the dog, by measured pace, never was farther than five long strides in front of his master. The dog didn't quarter, he just walked in a straight line five yards head of his two-legged companion through the cover. When I suggested that the dog was flushing birds the man would flush anyhow, I was greeted with a glance usually reserved for those who make obscene remarks to church-going maidens and country parsons. My companion was un-impressed by the fact that I, working alone and alongside this duo, flushed three more birds in a morning's hunt than they did. Old Tar was the greatest thing on four legs, and I must be a sorehead over missing so many.

Maybe so. And, I guess, with a Lab that flushes rather than points and holds the birds, working close enough to be seen is important. But, quartering the cover would have given the shooter better shots and more shots. As it was, if you wanted the dog down in the thick stuff, the owner had to walk down into it too, with the mutt leading the way. If the owner stayed on the high ground, so did the dog.

But this is the way, it seems, with woodcock dogs and their owners. Woodcock make a dog look SO good, that owners tend to overlook faults. It's a lot like the New York Yankees taking on the local slow pitch softball team. Even the guys who ride pine for the Yanks hit like the Babe and make the competition look sick. Thus it is with woodcock and dogs.

For instance, I hunt sometimes without a dog, and sometimes tend to shoot actually better than I do when I've got a dog along. The reason? The point gets my heart pounding, and my resolve and courage become the consistency of gelatin. I choke and clutch up. When I flush the birds myself, with no anticipation, I shoot better because there's no time to tighten up.

Of course, none of the preceding should be interpreted to come out that I don't think woodcock need dogs. Woodcock need dogs like turkey needs cranberry sauce, and quail need the Democrat wagon and a matched brace of mules. It's part of the tradition. In addition, woodcock shooting is far more productive with a GOOD dog, because the bird's tendency to sit it out means you'll walk past plenty of them without one.

What, then, is the purpose of a woodcock dog? I think the purpose is actually threefold. First off, the dog should be able to find and pin birds that you would not find without him, and be able to hold the birds there until you get there, not getting anxious and flushing them himself.

To do this, the dog should range widely through the cover, with only a small bell tinkling to give notice of his whereabouts. The dog should circle back every now and again to "check in" with the shooter, but mostly the animal should be out there in the cover, combing the corners that you can't reach, or don't want to. Then, when the bell stops, the dog is located, the flush made, and the dog is handy to be roundly cursed if the shot is missed.

The second thing the dog should do is retrieve or at least help you find the downed ones. There has been a lot of friendly ribbing, joking, and hilarity about dogs that won't fetch or even touch a downed woodcock, and plenty of talk about the ones that will lay a dead 'cock on the ground, but not retrieve it. But, it's damned maddening to lose a dead bird when you know just about where it came down because the dog won't help.

In reality, this should be one of the dog's primary functions. I hate losing birds and valuable hunting time because the dog has never been trained to retrieve the birds. I don't know how a dog can find and point a healthy 'cock, but refuse to even give you a hint of the whereabouts of a dead one, but they do it. Tracy, the dog in the first part of this chapter, would point live ones, catch and fetch wing-tipped birds, and nuzzle dead ones, but she'd only bring back dead ones if you made her, and we did.

Force training a dog to retrieve means the dog will retrieve EVERY time, regardless of the species or conditions, provided training isn't overly harsh. Birds that are airwashed as they fall are hard to find, but eventually enough scent will be given off for the dog to locate it. It's a matter of insisting, and not putting up with any nonsense.

I once hunted with a pointer that had a good scam going. If you downed a bird, she'd give the ground a once-over, often walking right over the dead bird. While we yelled and screamed, the dog capered around, ignoring the prostrate quarry. Then, when we'd get real serious about the whole thing, she'd trundle off a few yards and false point, drawing us over there in expectation of either a cripple or another bird. Her strategy was obviously to give us something new to think about so we'd quit bothering her about the dead bird she could smell and see nearby. The sight of her owner cutting an alder switch usually got her right back in the groove.

Why was this happening? Because the owner may have given up trying to make her fetch, would find the bird himself, and follow the dog into the cover where the mutt was already starting to hunt again. Gently insisting a puppy is to learn to retrieve and sticking to it is the only way to have a finished woodcock dog. Any dog that won't retrieve woodcock is not worthy of the name "woodcock dog." There are plenty of them.

Usually, this can be done by playfully building up the enthusiasm by making a game of fetching. An old woodcock wing, or a dead bird thrown and fetched as part of yard training would go a long way toward alleviating the non-retrieval bit. Sure, woodcock don't taste good, and maybe the feathers

DO come out in the dog's mouth, but there is no excuse for not retrieving. If the dog won't fetch, teach him to and keep at it—you're bigger and (hopefully) smarter than he is. Make him realize that you aren't going to hunt—that the fun stops—until the bird is found, and that's that!

One way is by pulling the wool over the dog's eyes a bit. By making the dog pick up the ones even YOU can see, eventually he'll think this is part of the job, and do it quickly so he can continue hunting. If you pick up the ones you find, but want help when you can't locate them, the dog probably won't help. So you've got to make the dog think that you know where EVERY bird is EVERY time, and you don't want any back sass about it.

Sometimes, the dogs will do some things you wish were recorded on film. Once, a bird flushed between my partner, Mark Sutton, and I. The shot was one of those eye-level chances, twisting through the aspen. I fired and the bird folded up. I heard Sutton's victory yelp, and knew that we'd fired at the same instant, my shot drowning the sound from his and vice versa.

Naturally, I quickly set him straight about who shot the bird, but he claimed I couldn't have seen the bird, and my shooting that day was proof that I couldn't have hit it if I had.

Well, Tracy seemed to sense the problem, and promptly brought the bird to Sutton. The retrieve itself—without insistence—was remarkable, but imagine our suprise when she sprinted out into the cover and delivered a second bird to me! There had been two, and she figured that we'd never know it unless she did something unusual, which she did.

Another time, I folded up a 'cock as it topped some alders. Search as we might, neither Sutton, Tracy nor myself could find a sign of the bird, just some wind-drifted feathers. Tracy kept coming over to where I was standing and looking up into my face. Sutton was near cardiac arrest from cursing the dog, and she even seemed to weary of staring at me and leaned against an alder trunk, her gaze still fixed on me. Finally, I moved a few steps, but her eyes didn't follow me. Tracing the line of her stare, I saw the bird wedged in the crotch of an alder, less than two feet from where I'd been standing. I swear that if the dog had claws long enough, she would have climbed the tree and brought it down. This is the only time I've ever seen a dog point UP, and the last time since.

Now, having said all of this on retrieving, I admit a nice compromise is keeping a Lab at heel to fetch birds killed over the points of the pointer, setter, or Brit. It works great, and you get to see two dogs' work.

The third purpose of a woodcock dog is to be a companion to the hunter. Because good woodcock dogs are more common than good grouse or pheasant dogs, the hunter is allowed to follow his fancy a bit more with respect to breed and coloring. I like a dog with a lot of white because he can be located in the cover better once the bell stops tinkling. Male or female matters little, although the bitch is usually a bit more methodical and tractable than the dog. Besides, if she's good, most of your friends will want to buy a pup, which makes for a little extra cash for peach brandy and applejack.

Of the pointing breeds, the setter, Brittany, and pointer are the most popular, with the German shorthair a close fourth. Flushing breeds that do well on 'cock are the springer, Lab, golden, and even the cocker spaniel.

On a whim, I even took my beagle woodcock hunting for the heck of it, and he found birds. But, woodcock hunting is a traditional sport, and tradition dictates the pointing breeds. Besides, many 'cock covers will hold grouse, and the pointing dogs work these birds better.

When shooting over dogs, yours or those of others, there are a few rules to be followed. Since woodcock hunting is a civilized sport, shots can be alternated, turns taken. When it's your shot, approach from the side rather than from behind. This makes the dog less nervous because he can see you and knows about when things are going to go BOOM. Also, the bird has fewer escape routes. By approaching the place the bird lies at a 90-degree angle from the dog, you've taken away another 90 degrees the bird can use to escape. He will rarely flush back toward the dog or toward you, which leaves you either with a straight away shot or a left or right hand crossing shot, depending on which way you approach the dog.

This is also a good way to cheat on your shooting. Let's say that you have a hard time with right-to-left crossers. If so, approach from the angle that will mean the bird must flush going away, or left to right. This would be to approach with the dog staunch and on your left. This leaves only your better shots as the most likely possibility.

Of course, about the time you try this, the birds will start flushing right straight at you, their wing wash breezing your face, and all bets are off.

All of this talk is well and good, but what of the dog that just refuses to hunt woodcock? Simple. Save him for other game or give him away to a good home. Woodcock days are too short, and the season too flawless for spoiling the hours afield with an uncooperative dog. Most dogs that won't hunt 'cock were introduced to the bird late in life, after their habits were formed. I've never seen a dog started on the birds young that wasn't an eager hunter.

In fact, there's a lot to be said for woodcock when it comes to stretching the days a dog has afield. When the spring is gone from a dog's step, and he can't keep up with racing ringnecks or grouse, he can still plod along enough to do a good job on woodcock. The covers are usually small and intimate, the weather superb, and the rest periods lengthy because of the lazy weather, so take the old boy woodcock hunting. He'll love it.

In a lot of ways, I guess, the same can be said for the human hunter, and his days afield, which in opportunity and years, are all too few.

Steve Smith

Woodcock Dogs

I'm sort of bent in the direction of being a woodcock dog man. I have a greater sympathy for them than for dogs that can race the wind and win over a Texas plain or a prairie ocean. I'm probably due to come back as a woodcock dog if there's such a thing as reincarnation (in spite of deserving to come back as a distance fly-casting champion or a frequent high-over-all winner on the high-rolling trap circuit), but I have a feeling that that's not in the cards.

Woodcock dogs and I have a basic and instant understanding. No doubt it started when I was a yearling gunner just past being housebroken. If I flushed a bird in those beginning years, I was the one who flushed it—intentionally or not. I spent so much time in the bottom covers and alder thickets that I got relatively good at the whole game. I can't claim a choke-bore nose, but I did have a pretty good feeling for where a bird or so might lie, and I did better, given my overeagerness and inadequate wingshooting technique, than you might suppose.

No one in his right mind would have counted on me to produce a limit; no one would have preferred my company to that of all but the most ancient or hopeless bird dogs, but all I had was me, and that had to do. In my favor, if memory isn't being too generous with the facts, was a thick-headedness that no cover could deter. No bramble was too dense, no swamp too wet, no hillside too steep. If it looked or felt or hinted at being birdy, I would plunge right on. I must have flushed—unknown, unseen, and unheard by me—hundreds for every

one I threw a rather random load of light 8's at, but my options were just two: my way or nothing.

Aside from being a less-than-spectacular wingshot, combined with a certain lack of stealth, I had other shortcomings that even I was aware of: one was the fact that I was slightly hard of hearing—it runs in the family—and another was that I was short. Where a boy of normal size, equipped with better ears than I, would have heard or seen a bird, I was destined to plunge on unrewarded by not even having a glimpse of tawny feathers or the reward of whirring wings and the faint whistle that woodcock so often make when flushed.

You don't have to be "Nick the Greek" or an old hand from Vegas to figure the odds on a short, slightly deaf, noisy boy sneaking up on enough birds to provide much of a family feast. That I did get enough birds every season to keep my interest at a ridiculously high level has to say something about the number of birds in my old coverts any my ability to play a little loose with the facts about my hunting skills. You could put me down as some kind of an unreasonable optimist; what does it cost you to be kind?

"Years later," as they used to head chapters in old novels, the boy has grown somewhat taller and a lot more circumspect about ramming headfirst through the greenbriars. Constant pipe smoking has taken the edge off his wind and a little practice has brought him up a shade from the absolute dregs of shotgun pointing. He has, by this time, read a great deal more on the sport, and has had an opportunity or two to gun behind a four-legged bird dog; while not a fountain of lore, he is way past where we last saw him—peering upward through short brush with one hand cupped behind his better ear. While his skills and his eagerness are still incredibly far apart, he shows signs of promise.

In time, as you have no doubt guessed, he acquires a bird dog. A nice dog. A dog who likes him and vows to do her best. A dog who thoroughly enjoys wallowing in the mud of bottom covers, creeping through alders, and jogging in the relative open of birches. A perfect match, this man and dog; for although willing to please, she is somewhat cold-nosed, a touch hard of hearing, and irritatingly stubborn. But they find more birds together than he ever did alone (not all that many by more reasonable standards, but a definite improvement has taken place).

Well, more dogs come and go. Shotguns are traded, skeet and trap guns are acquired. His circle of gunning companions grows. The time actually arrives when he has a biddable, knowing bird dog. His clay target scores are not the lowest in the club every Sunday. He has lost little or none of his fondness for creekside covers, and the pungent odors of the bog country are still as attractive as ever. He has matured, at least as much as a woodcock hunter ever does.

He is at the time of his life where the coming season is anticipated as much for the little picture it will leave him to pleasure over as it is for the actual gunning itself. He remembers what October smells like as early as August. He pleasures himself by imagining the coming opening day to be a bit on the crisp side and it having rained heavily about four or five days before—to clear the air, to damp the bottoms and to thin the leaves.

He remembers an evening bird he saw the last time out in late November past. He remembers swinging through its flight with an empty 20-gauge, a limit of woodcock snugging his shooting vest comfortably tight across his shoulders. He even imagines that he heard it whistle.

He sits and recalls a very special Pennsylvania hillside where he was gunning with an old man and his long-time setter friend—both out against all common sense and at least one of them against his doctor's orders. Standing a bit above the pair, he watched the tottering dog work out the puzzles of a fist-tight bird in a soft and shifting breeze. When she had it absolutely right, the setter stopped, holding her head high, proud, and elegant. The old man walked over, shuffled the leaves with his boot, and watched the woodcock shuttle up through the trees.

"Forget the safety, Carl?" came the watcher's voice from up on the hillside.

"You'd think I'd know better, wouldn't you, after all these years," answered the man down in the swale.

The man on the hillside, the watcher, didn't say anything more. He knew better, too—after all these years.

He delights in that picture. It's his absolute favorite—so far. He wonders, rather idly, if anything nearly that sweet is likely to occur this coming season. He knows, now, that it doesn't matter at all.

Gene Hill

Memories of
Misses Past

It's sort of traditional at the end of the year to look back and take stock of what has happened during the last 12 months. One friend of mine keeps a diary. The regular kind, you might have seen one, for hunters and shooters. But a diary is pretty matter-of-fact. You sit around with a couple of your shooting buddies and one of them says, "... that was the day you had the double on green-wing teal ..." Without a diary you can agree and return the compliment with something along the line of "... yes, that's right; I remember it well because it was just two weeks later *you* had a 94 at Grouse Ridge Gun Club ..." and the evening is warm with the passing of such soft and sweet memories. But with a diary this never happens. The diary reveals that not only did you not double up on green-wing teal on that particular day (you did not one time double on anything, all year), you missed four easy incomers flaring out over the decoys and went home with two sea ducks. The diary would also reveal that George M. did not get a 94. The diary would read that as usual George M. was stopping his gun and lucked into an 87. The diary is to the shooter as the scale and the tape measure are to the fisherman—irrefutable proof that the judgment and memory of the outdoorsman improves, like a fine wine, with the passing of time. We're not in the business of facts and figures, anyway. Nobody's keeping score. Our end of the year inventory can have anything on the shelf we want. Two ruffed grouse can become eight or even ten or twelve. If you count the near misses, perhaps even a trifle more. The weather along the Chesapeake can get a lot colder and windier when you're sitting in front of a log fire a month later.

So instead of taking a long, hard look at the times gone by, let's take a softer dreamy one. Why not put your feet up on the good furniture and see what you'd like to have happened. This is nowhere near any form of lying—that's an art in itself. We're just looking at the truth from a variety of angles. Did Old Ben break into a covey of birds and flush them out of sight or do you suspect that he hit a running bunch of birds and did damn well to put them up so you could mark down the singles?

Did you really miss that huge old gander that came sailing in on set wings or did you just fire way behind him on purpose—sort of a parting salute? Did you really end up with only a 17 on your last round of trap or were you "working" with the gun to test the width of the pattern? Give it a little thought and you'll discover some nice smooth lines to shore up your story. I know one shooter who can barely hit the ground with his hat and after his usual two-shot miss he waves his gun barrel around very happily and says "Boy, that's what I'm out here for . . . just to see 'em fly!" He's carried on like this for so long that even *I'm* tempted to believe him. Trapshooters who have a long string of zeros will talk about how they're just polishing timing and rhythm. And one of the stupidest bird dogs I have ever seen is constantly praised by his owner for his "range."

So, look back and see what fits—from a different perspective. And next year start giving your Christmas presents early. Comment in admiration on some shooter's rhythm and timing. Slap your buddy on the back next time his dog busts every bird for a square mile and tell him how much you hate those close-working dogs that are always right there almost under your feet. And when we're together and it's one of those days when I'm a little bit off, it would be a kind thing for us to chat about sportsmanship and the bigger meaning of being out-of-doors.

Gene Hill

Shooting Logs

Although not all grouse and woodcock hunters will agree, I think that the season can be more meaningful, the good times can be made more lasting, and much can be learned about the birds and those who seek them through the use of a shooting log, or an "upland diary" if you please.

Essentially, the shooting log book is a series of notes that are recorded shortly after each hunt so that you can look back on them during the off season to learn a few things about your chosen sport.

For example, you may find that you are gunning a particular cover too often, or that your shooting percentage was better on days when you got the most points (no surprise here), or that the birds moved best when the weather was a bit breezy from the southwest.

The log, as I keep mine, is in a loose-leaf notebook, the kind you used to carry to school when you really wanted to be out in the woods somewhere instead of listening to Miss Priss teaching you to conjugate your verbs.

The loose-leaf paper contained therein holds the following information: date, partner with whom I hunted, weather conditions, time of day we started and stopped, covers we hunted, number and species of birds moved, number of flushes, number of birds bagged at each cover, and how I personally shot that day.

Naturally, a series of codes are set up so that I can save time in making my entries, but a lot of the information is transferred to numbers during the off season. I do this because I like to think about grouse and woodcock all year long, and this gives me a chance to do just that.

For example, I note the total number of birds moved, and flushes made in each cover, and transfer this information to a file box which contains the names of all the covers I hunt. This information tells me which of my covers is becoming less productive in terms of the number of birds moved; usually this happens as a cover ages.

Keeping track of individual birds moved is actually easier than it sounds, even with woodcock, which will normally present a large number of flushes in a single day in any of your covers compared to grouse. Obviously, you subtract the number of dead birds—those you've bagged—from the total birds in a given cover. By keeping track of the birds as they flush, it's pretty easy to tell if a bird flushed is a reflush or a new bird. If you flush five birds and shoot two of them, then you know the cover held at least two birds. If you've flushed birds AFTER the two were shot, then you know there is at least another bird in there. By watching reflushes and being conservative, you can come up with a surprisingly accurate number of birds. Short of shooting every bird every time, which nobody ever should or could, this is the best way to count them.

The shooting log also tells, as indicated earlier, which days prove to be the best in which types of cover. For example, those absolute bluebird days show me that the 'cock are usually found on the sunny hillsides, as are grouse. Windy days 'cock are in thicker cover—usually aspen/alder association, and grouse will flush wild. However, most of my really good woodcock shooting has been done on these windy days, producing great action—but damned tricky shots. This works out fine because grouse are tough to find on windy days.

I keep track of productive points, not for any good reason, but just to have something to fiddle with where dogs are concerned, and I also note where the finds were made. Some covers produce a number of good points, and some offer birds as targets only after the dog or the hunter has bumped them. I don't know why. Maybe someday I'll figure it out. It must be in the topography or the way the scent lies close to the ground or something.

My tabulation also tells me which covers hold a sizeable population of grouse, which have mainly woodcock, and which are true combination covers. Naturally, I visit the grouse covers later, when the little russet sprites have headed south. During the 'cock season, I gun almost nothing else. They're gone too soon as it is.

Another thing that is suggested by the log is which woodcock covers are early and late season covers. In some states, like Michigan, the season opens in mid-September. Because of this early opening, there are covers that hold native birds only, those which nested there. I try to steer clear of these, preferring to shoot birds when they are migrating, thus avoiding overtaxing the native flocks in my covers. My log tells me that some covers are used only during measurable migration, and the approximate dates.

The log has also told me where the birds are found during wet years, dry years, times of the day and so on. The memory is a convenient thing. The log seldom lies. Even though the log may appear impartial, cold, and calculating, it is useful, expands your fun, and is a great learning process.

Now, dear friend, comes the part that—once committed to paper in your log—becomes part of the annals of your personal history: the shooting average. Over the years, shooters, particularly grouse and woodcock hunters, have come up with convenient memories regarding their own prowess with a smoothbore. The reason for this is obvious. On some days, the angelic hosts are smiling benevolently upon us from afar. We are blessed with a series of straightaways, none of which fly into the sun, and your favorite Parker works in perfect harmony with your legendary muscular coordination. Your limit of four birds is sacked with that many right barrels.

On other days, nature and a poor digestion conspire to rob you of anything even remotely resembling a decent chance. The briars grab you as you turn to fire. The alders slap you upside the head just as you try to mount the gun. The wind comes up and every bird flushes wild, turns with the wind, and flies so fast that enough forward allowance is impossible. Leaves are sucked off the trees by the wind created from the passing of the birds, so great is their speed. On such days, the damned dog insists on trying to leap on every bird that should be pointed. You brought the wrong shot size, and your partner happens to be on a hot streak, which, naturally, adds to the problems.

We know, don't we, that such days are few and far between, minor lapses in an otherwise perfect record of flawless marksmanship with the shotgun? Or are they?

Only a shooting diary can tell you if this is so. Now, for the faint of heart who are afraid that the outcome will be not quite to their liking, let me make a suggestion. Keep the record for two years. If the second year's average is not better or is indeed worse that the first year's, then discontinue the practice. Brand it and me stupid, inane, and detracting from the spirit of the hunt, and let it go at that.

If, however, you find that the second season's tally looks better than your first season's figure, you'll be so pleasantly surprised that you'll want to continue.

Now, exactly how does one keep such a record of fine deeds with the shotgun? Very simply, save your empty shells, count them at the end of the day, and count your birds. Factor out all shells fired at grouse and count these separately from those shells fired at woodcock.

At the end of the season, check the entries in your log where you should have entered the day's shooting success with a: "Grouse—two for six; Woodcock—three for twelve" type of statement, and start doing the arithmetic. Since my daughter, Amy, is better at this than I, she tells me that during the last three seasons on woodcock I shot 31% (bad knee that year, and my stock portfolio was in trouble) my first year of shooting average records. I rose to 56% the second year (more in keeping with my native skill, stealth, and Midwestern cunning) and the latest season was 68%. I may quit keeping records of my shooting, and from now on tell people that I average two woodcock for every three shells fired. If next season's average drops, I'll do just that.

On grouse, I shot 23%, 32%, and 40% for these same three years—only the last year is really acceptable, but I'm getting better.

I also keep a separate little section that tells about each grouse and 'cock I shoot. The information recorded includes: cover in which the bird was taken, range (paced off), which barrel, gun and load, and type of shot. Here I classify them as straightaway, rising, quartering away right, quartering away left, and so forth. With this, I can tell which are my best shots, and therefore get an idea about how to lie, connive, or otherwise hoodwink my shooting partner into letting me work the side of the cover where these shots will be most likely.

For example, I'm scared to death of a low, left to right crosser, something you often get on windy days. Because of this, I make sure that I hunt on the left, and so any low crossers are more likely to be right to left, on which I do a bit better.

The section with this information also tells me that the birds tend to fly certain ways on certain days due to weather conditions.

For example, I've found that 'cock most often go out low, fast, and darting when the weather is overcast, or late in the day. Being crepuscular, the birds probably see best at this time. Not being crepuscular, I see lousy at this time, and my shooting on such birds shows it.

On bluebird days, with what we used to call a "high sky" in my baseball days, little or no cloud activity and a gentle breeze, the birds don't fly in such a peppy manner. These days I get my share. As a matter of fact, maybe that's why I like such days so well, I can hit 'em then!

My log tells me that grouse are feeding actively before a snowstorm, and that wind puts them up out of range, usually. A light steady rain makes the birds hold a bit better, and scenting is very good. A steady downpour, however, and the birds are likely to be in the thick stuff, trying to keep dry. Early morning is usually not good late in the season, because the birds seem to want to wait for the frost to come off before venturing off the roosting sites. Late evening, just at sundown, often produces the best shooting of the day where open cover joins thick stuff as the birds congregate a bit to feed and get ready to roost.

Had enough about paper work? Not so fast. How about maps? The topographical maps, discussed in other chapters are invaluable in locating covers, and can also point out some other likely spots for you to check out, so keep these handy and use them.

In addition, most counties sell plat maps, available through the local Soil Conservation District for about five bucks. These show the names of the owners of every parcel of land in the county, township by township. This can be especially useful in two ways. The first way is in locating public land. In many parts of the country, especially the Midwest, not all public lands are marked as public, and most are open to hunting if you only knew where they were. With the plat map, you can locate a 40-acre section here, a corner there, that are owned by the state or some municipality, and can be hunted without prior permission.

It's interesting to note that some of these parcels are often posted up tight. Seems some of the local gents know the lands are public, but post them against "trespass" by outsiders. Some even go so far as to throw you off their little usurped domains. A few seasons back, I was surprised to find a rather irate fellow waiting by my Jeep, obviously upset that I had chosen to hunt on posted land.

"Can't you read?" he rudely inquired, pointing toward one of the signs. I replied that I wasn't smoking, but he saw little humor in this.

"This land is posted, and you're trespassing!" he ranted. "Now, get off and don't come back."

Uneasily casing my Ithaca, I reached into the glove box of the vehicle and pulled out my trusty plat book, dialed the right township and section, and calmly observed that my conversant must be the State of Michigan, the owner of this land.

He wanted a look at my little book, decided he'd had enough, and walked off. I, naturally, removed all the signs. They were not put up again that season or the next.

The second way the plat book comes in handy is in asking permission to hunt if the area you have chosen is on private land. Now, let me parenthetically say that getting permission to shoot woodcock only is usually met with peals of laughter. Close blood relatives are often summoned to get a first hand look at the imbecile who would want to hunt these little creatures. Of course, it is usually easy to convince the landowner that all you are after is the 'cock, not his pet covey of grouse, or the pheasants that still haunt the place. Also, explain that you can tell the difference between a woodcock and a cow. But, it is certainly more helpful if you know the owner's name beforehand to open the conversation. Getting the name off the mailbox is fine, provided it's there, but the plat map always tells. If you can use the owner's name, you have a better chance of success.

By the way, beware the notations on the map. I once inquired at a house if I could speak with Mr. Et. al for permission to hunt, because that's what the map said, C. Jones, Et. al. Unfortunately, he wasn't in at the time.

Getting permission to hunt the more popular grouse is greatly aided by knowing the owner's name beforehand. My log also records names and addresses of such people. I send them Christmas cards to keep channels open, and I've made quite a few friends and shooting contacts this way.

As we all know too well, the shooting season has to end sometime, and that time usually is about when we get the kinks worked out of our legs, or just break out of that shooting slump. The problem, then, is how to stretch the season so that it can last all year. Let me offer some suggestions which you may find helpful when grouse and woodcock withdrawal symptoms set in.

One way is to take a shooting vacation in the South. Louisiana, Georgia, the Carolinas and the other Southern states have large wintering populations of woodcock, and they are largely underhunted. The local gunners prefer quail, and many a good "bird" dog has been disposed of on the open market because of a predilection for pointing woodcock. A few boxes of shells, a good snakebite kit, and a few free days are all that's required to enjoy some good Southern shooting, cooking, and hospitality.

Another way, barring this or in addition to it, is to join

one of the clubs devoted to improving the lot of the grouse and woodcock.

The Ruffed Grouse Society has local chapters, newsletters, banquets and other get-togethers to ease the burden of hanging up the shotgun for another year. Getting together to swap lies with others of a similar cut does wonders for a shooter's nerves, and the work it does managing land is a bonus for the birds and for the bird hunters.

Working the dogs, where legal, in good bird covers is exhilarating and a sport unto itself. You can be out in the field, check out new covers in the process, and maybe nip some bad habits that Old Missy developed during the gunning season, but you overlooked because you were interested in shooting and not dog training.

Annually, Mark Sutton and I set aside a weekend in late July for this purpose, and have a good time in the process. We can keep tabs on the birds, and scout new covers. As grouse and woodcock covers age, they grow beyond their productive years. Pre-season scouting tells us if any of our pet covers are at this point.

If you own some land, or maybe have access to private acreage, you could carry out some of the management plans that are outlined later in this book. It is a rather simple matter to lease private land in good grouse country for hunting rights. Usually, an absentee landholder is happy to give such rights in exchange for payment of the annual property taxes. In some parts of the country, this is tough, but throughout good grouse and woodcock range, not impossible.

In fact, more and more grouse/'cock hunting clubs are springing up. Similar to deer and duck camps, these places feature private acreage, managed for grouse and 'cock, with the membership having access to other acreage. In some states, the seasons are much longer than the seasons for other game, so these camps make sense from a usage standpoint. Shop around in the off season for such places.

While you're shopping around in the off season, get permission to hunt on private land. It is much easier in August than on opening morning. Carry a pad of paper with you, and record the owner's signature so there's no problem later on.

It's nice to know that you have a place to hunt when you roll out on opening morning.

Lastly, why not get right out into the field and study the habits of these birds? Listening for drumming by grouse, and watching the evening song of the woodcock during mating is a beautiful and soul-cleansing experience. It gives you tips on some places to hunt the next fall, and helps you understand the quarry better. The years I spent studying fall migration of woodcock were golden indeed, much of it done without the gun, but always with respect for the bird.

Sometimes the shooting diary will reveal that you made a poor choice of companions for a day afield. In my early days, I'd go shooting with anybody who'd ask me along. I got a raw deal many times. Safety, naturally, is of the utmost concern to all good shooters, and I'll not belabor the point of proper shooting and gun handling safety here. Suffice it to say that you'll never shoot another person or yourself or a dog if the gun never points at them. As a point of courtesy, I always break open my gun, even if only stopping to catch my breath or when conversing about which way to work a cover before continuing.

However, sportsmanship is often overlooked more and more as the numbers of birds dwindle and places to hunt become fewer.

I am not a deer hunter. I have nothing against this fine sport, and realize the need for scientifically managed and controlled harvesting of this animal. What I don't like is the fact that there is usually a red shirt behind each tree, and crowds usually breed unsporting attitudes. I go hunting to get away from the city crowds, not to join them in the woods.

Over the years, I have narrowed my list of companions to a very few. They are men who I trust with my life, quite literally, and they trust me likewise. Mark Sutton, the fellow mentioned in several places in this book is one such man, so is his brother, Neil. My kid brother, Eric—he of the practical jokes—is another. Having saved my life once years ago with a fancy bit of mouth-to-mouth resusitation, I'm sure he'd not accidentally take it now.

There are a few others, but they all have one thing in common: The gun is never pointed at me or anyone else. It is always—even in a head over heels fall down a creek bank—pointed safely.

But above this point, the true sporting companion is the kind of gentleman who will rib you unmercifully about blowing an easy shot, but will offer you a point if he has a bird more than you or has had more shots.

He will insist that a bird is yours if you should fire at the same time and thus "double" on the same bird. Mark and I do this at least twice a year, and split up the results accordingly—each claiming a hit for shooting average computation—but offering the other the bird.

Keeping one's word about hunting commitments is important. Though a small consideration, it is a good idea to make sure that new shooting acquaintances agree on starting times, quitting times, and how hard they wish to hunt.

I once hunted with a gent who sounded like a real red-hot brush-popper, the kind who goes at every opportunity. When I swung by to pick him up at his house about 7 A.M., he was still asleep. After he rummaged around and found his hunting stuff (which could have been done the night before) he sat at his kitchen table and drank six cups of black coffee while I fidgeted. Finally arriving at the shooting grounds, two hours later than I'd planned, we hunted for three hours when he announced that we had to leave. He had to get back because he wanted to watch the telecast of the local college game, and besides he didn't like to hunt any longer than a few hours anyway. Believe me, he got taken home at above legal speed limits, and I went back to hunt.

Another time, I made an arrangement to hunt with a man who professed to know little of grouse shooting, but wanted to learn. I arrived at his house at the usual 7 A.M. hour, and he was all ready to go, gear and gun stowed on his back porch. As I loaded his stuff in the trunk, he said we couldn't leave just yet because his brother-in-law and his three boys and a friend of one of the boys hadn't arrived yet. Seems he'd invited those souls along once our date was set. I developed a sudden attack of the stomach flu, and took my leave, never to hunt with him again.

Later, a friend told me this was standard practice with this guy and that this is how he located his covers. He'd get someone to take him, produce his entourage, and they'd all have a fine day in the field shooting the host's birds. Usually, the host lost his covers, which they quickly despoiled by overshooting, and they had to find another sucker. It happened to be my turn.

In the field itself, there are a few types to watch out for. The bird claimer feels he hits every bird he shoots at, and if he can see them, he's going to shoot, even if it's your bird because of the direction of the flush. This character can be dangerous. You'll never cure him, so avoid him. Don't try to appeal to his better nature by giving him every bird he claims, because it won't work—he has no better nature.

The drinker is another that is frustrating and dangerous to be out with. First off, he wants to stop at every bar on the way up and back, and may try to pick up a little feminine companionship at every stop. He usually totes his booze into the field with him, and disposes of the empties wherever fancy directs. In addition, he's damned dangerous, even if he only wants a beer every hour or so. His judgment and reflexes are impaired.

I've been known to nip the grape now and again, but not while I'm hunting or about to hunt. At the day's end, fine. Not before.

The game stealer is another type to avoid like he was carrying Bubonic toxin. This kind will pick up a bird you've shot and pocket it without your knowledge, claiming you missed. Later on, he'll take a shot when screened by cover and claim a bird. Now his shell/bird/ratio is right. One guy did this to me, the only time it's ever happened that I know of. He claimed I missed a woodcock, one I thought I was on just as it ducked behind a clump of witchhazel. Later, he pulled the shoot-in-the-air routine.

However, he didn't know I was beginning to study woodcock that season and was surprised when I asked to see it for sexing and aging purposes. The woodcock he produced had the early stages of rigor mortis. I sexed it, aged it, and pocketed it without a word. He didn't protest.

Still another type is the fellow who has hunted with you for some time before his character flaw rears its head. This guy will know, after a cover has been hunted several times, where the birds are most likely to be, and positions himself accordingly.

In most covers I hunt, this is difficult, because as you progress sometimes the choice spots are on the right, sometimes on the left, so both men get an equal chance. This isn't good enough. When the good cover is on the right, so is our Champion Positioner. When the good, productive upcoming cover is on the left, our pal calls a halt for a smoke and a breather. As we start off again, he's now on the left, and you are out in the unproductive stuff. Slick.

One man I shot with some years back was great at this, and I finally figured it out. I asked him if it would help if I left my gun in the car and just went along to watch and play dog. He reddened in the face, and that was our last hunting trip. Mutual parting of the ways.

Although it's all too uncommon, the overly courteous companion is almost as bad. This chap wants to make sure that you get shooting, so he passes up his share of the points, passes up shots at birds, waiting for you to shoot, and even takes frequent halts to let you rest. Such a man is trying to be a sportsman, but he doesn't know how. I much prefer a man who takes his chances as they come, shares everything, and doesn't make me feel like I'm depriving him of sport. I feel more comfortable knowing he wants to get birds too, and isn't out there as my guide only.

I think woodcock shooting promotes the better sportsmanship because chances come more often than with grouse. Besides, grouse are usually considered better table fare by most and are sought more keenly. A man who dismisses 'cock as unhittable will scratch your eyes out for a shot at a grouse—at least that's my experience.

Steve Smith

Grouse and
Woodcock Management

Game management for ruffed grouse, throughout his range, remains minimal when compared to other, perhaps more popular species, such as white-tail deer. However, management itself for these birds is not difficult, and luckily takes little land. A thriving population of birds can be raised on as little as 10 acres, provided all elements are present, but a parcel 40 acres or larger is more suitable.

For the gunner, especially one with no land of his own to carry out these practices, the question may be asked "Where the hell do I get the land?"

Deer clubs often have large landholdings, and are not adverse to managing for grouse, because good grouse management is good deer management. Land can be leased for the taxes and management set up to help grouse and woodcock, and the reader of this book may even be contemplating a land purchase of his own with an eye toward improving grouse populations.

With that in mind, let's examine the elements that make up good grouse management. Since the grouse is a bird of the edges, it will be necessary to create these edges artificially if they don't exist on the land at the beginning of management procedures. The chain saw is the tool that is used here. Hopefully, the vegetation of any parcel of land set aside for grouse will have a large population of aspen trees. These trees are almost a weed throughout much grouse range, and grow quickly. The aspen come in various species, but the most common are the Largetooth Aspen (*Populus gradidentata*) and the Quaking Aspen (*Populus tremuloides*). These trees live about 45 years, but grow brittle and are subject to heartwood rot after about 25 years. We are interested in the aspen from its germination until it is about a quarter century.

With all plants, natural attrition takes place. The sun-tolerant aspen grows best in the open. In its own shade, new aspen trees cannot grow, so there is a gradual thinning of the aspen until new forest types come in, such as white pine (*Pinus stroba*) and the various species of maple, such as sugar maple (*A. saccharum*). Birch trees (*Betula papyrifera*) will grow with the aspen, and do not compete with them. Birch whips, in fact, will grow from the stumps of the tree if it is cut, and the birch is a nice source of firewood for the old clubhouse.

If left to its own devices, a forest will age through the aspen stage eventually to a stage involving the sugar maple and beech (*Fagus grandifolia*) association in the Northeast and upper Midwest. At this point, the forest is at the "climax," or terminal stage, and no new trees can survive because of the intense shade generated by these trees. Barring a fire or cutting, the beech/maple climax stage will endure forever, being succeeded only by its own kind. All other trees cannot tolerate the extreme shade conditions.

On the floor of a climax forest, little vegetation can flourish, and the shrub layer is virtually nonexistent, and therefore so is grouse cover. The idea, then, is to open the forest floor to sunlight, and to encourage the growth of grouse food and cover plants, either naturally or by direct planting of flora where it does not naturally occur.

As we saw in an earlier chapter, the grouse requires a variety of forest ages throughout its yearly cycle. Hardwoods are necessary because it is here that nesting takes place. The old hen builds her nest near an oak or maple tree for better protection, and her coloration blends so well with the dead leaves that she will actually cover herself with leaves during the early stages of incubation.

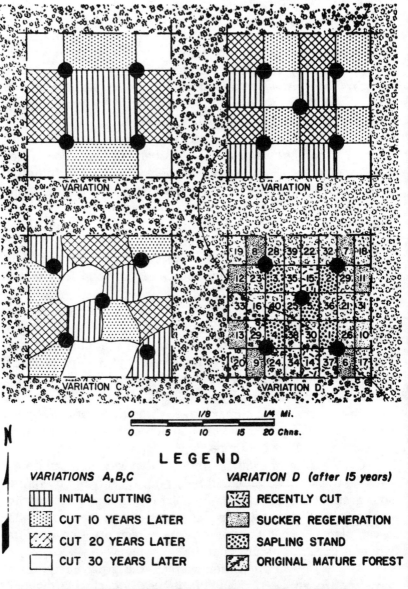

VARIATION A

VARIATION B

VARIATION C

VARIATION D

19	8	28	39	22	32	7	18
12	23	3	35	15	2	29	11
33	16	40	25	5	36	21	31
13	29	4	38	30	1	26	10
20	9	24	34	14	37	6	17

0   1/8   1/4 Mi.

0   5   10   15   20 Chns.

N

L E G E N D

VARIATIONS A,B,C

▦ INITIAL CUTTING

▦ CUT 10 YEARS LATER

▨ CUT 20 YEARS LATER

☐ CUT 30 YEARS LATER

VARIATION D (after 15 years)

▦ RECENTLY CUT

▦ SUCKER REGENERATION

▦ SAPLING STAND

▨ ORIGINAL MATURE FOREST

● EXPECTED CENTER FOR RUFFED GROUSE BREEDING
ACTIVITY FOLLOWING MANAGEMENT

OPTION I. A management prescription for a 40-year forest tract, showing four variations in treating the same sized area. In Variation A the blocks include a central one of 10 acres, and four each of 2½ acres and 5 acres; in Variation B all the blocks are 2½ acres in size; and those in Variation C are about 2½ acres each, except across the bottom. Each block in Variation D is 1 acre, with the numbers indicating the year in which that piece would be cut. Forest condition for this variation is shown as it would appear 15 years after management commenced.

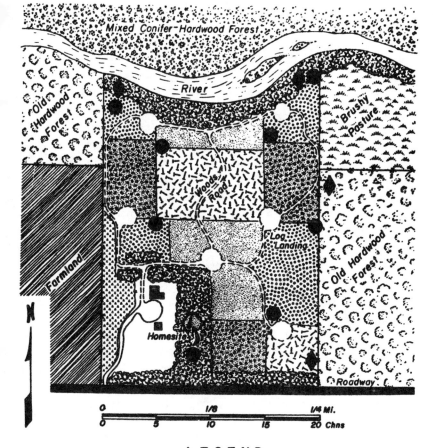

OPTION II. This shows how the Ruffed Grouse habitats on a 60-acre forest tract containing a home-site might be distributed 21 years after management began.

After the chicks are hatched, she seeks a large population of insects for her chicks, for the young birds—for the first 10 days of life or so—are voracious protein seekers, and protein means bugs. For this food source, the birds need young growth of aspen—up to eight years of age. These are really aspen whips—thousands of stems to the acre and resembling a bit-over-head-high jungle. Here, she and her young are safe from airborne predators, and the young scamper and forage.

As they age, the young birds seek other types of food, the berries and fruits of certain shrubs and bushes such as grapevines and blackberries, which also offer protection. These types are more common in a middle-aged stand of aspen, from 8 to 15 years of age. The stems are farther apart, due to the death of some trees because of inability to compete, and the birds stay in these areas throughout the summer and early fall. The shrub layer offers good cover as well as food, and it is here the autumn gunner seeks him.

Even though grouse rarely starve, they do get pinched for food in the winter, and then they seek the buds from the oldest aspen trees, those 25 years of age or more. The male aspen produces buds in the late fall, and carries them through the winter. A budding grouse will really load up on these nutricious morsels, and will seek shelter in conifers, such as cedar or spruce trees, thus warding off the energy-sapping winter winds.

We can see, then, that grouse require the planting of conifers, a hardwood stand for nesting, and aspen trees in three various stages of growth.

Besides this, the birds are helped along by plantings of such plants as dogwood, willows, viburnum, juneberry, wintergreen, clover, and a host of other plants. However, most of these will occur naturally in the forest once aspen trees are regulated to proper size and age.

The proper way to manage is to carry out all the procedures that follow within a 10 acre plot. If your land is larger than 10 acres, repeat each 10 acres. The maximum carrying capacity is one breeding pair per 10 acres. With good brood survival, this could mean up to 24 grouse per 40 acres—not bad!

First off, after examining the forest, you determine that the aspen must be cut to open the forest floor. Clear cut a one-acre section of land in an irregular pattern. This increases edge. About 50 yards away, repeat this procedure 10 years later. Ten years later, repeat a third one-acre area. The hardwoods should be left in the center of this area, and other planting of conifers should be made in or near the most mature stage, which is not the first clear cut acre.

In 10 years, go back and cut the oldest stand. It is now the youngest. The process is repeated each 10 to 12 years, always cutting the oldest stand so that it becomes the youngest. The youngest will become the middle-aged, and the middle-aged stand will be the oldest, until it is cut.

When planting conifers, plant them in blocks, leaving strips of openings between the blocks. These will naturally succeed also.

A water course of some type should be nearby, such as a swamp, stream, or lake edge. The birds will seek the lush vegetation that will grow here during dry summers.

The map shown with the description will aid in arranging all elements of management properly.

Woodcock Management

One of the things I'd hoped to do with the information I gathered was to try to formulate methods of managing for woodcock. I'm not sure how this can be done, yet, short of providing adequate cover for them in areas they are using anyway. Some states are attempting management now, with others planning to do so.

Probably the chainsaw would be the main tool for 'cock management. As shown earlier, when cover ages, it thins and thus offers less protection. As this thinning occurs and thick grasses grow, the birds move elsewhere. It would be, then, a matter of keeping the cover down to a size the birds prefer. With aspen, this is less than 15 years old and under 20 feet in height. Slow growing alders are less a problem, but they, too, should be cut back when it looks like they are too old, say over 15 feet high. By clear-cutting a small area here and there—about a quarter acre at a time—every five years or so, there will always be some area that is to the birds' liking. Naturally, none of this will do any good if the birds aren't using the area to begin with.

I'd also suggest that some area of an acre or two be kept completely clear-cut or the soil worked up all the time to provide the singing grounds the birds need in springtime.

In any event, much time and money must yet be expended before we can adequately manage for woodcock. Being migratory, the birds don't need the more extensive management devoted to grouse.

In states where deer management is carried out extensively, this also helps grouse and woodcock because it keeps the habitat in some stage of disturbance through cutting, and promotes the growth of edge cover. In addition, rabbits and other small mammals will thrive on such managed tracts.

On some land my rich father owns, merely cutting roads through mature stands of aspen has increased the bird population near the cuttings. An old cockbird drums and struts nearby, and coveys of young birds are often seen near the new roads, feeding on the vegetation that sprouted on these new edges.

As you are aware, there is a real energy crunch in this country, and aside from cutting down on the miles that the shooter can drive to hunt, the shortages are having other effects as well, so far just being felt.

Among these effects is the propensity of some citizens to cut their own firewood. Now, cutting your own firewood is great fun, provided somebody doesn't drop a tree on you. Cutting firewood puts you in the open air in the late summer or early fall—maybe even in the spring if you are the type who plans ahead. Secondly, cutting firewood really keeps you warm, and not just when you actually burn it. You get to sweat while you cut it, load it, unload it, split it, carry it into the house and finally tote out the ashes. You also get to watch the flames lick high in the fireplace and chuckle contentedly as the house thermostat stays off and the gnomes at the power company wring their hands wondering how they'll pay THEIR electric bills because you're short-changing them this winter.

Many states have realized that this modern day pioneer is a good source of cheap labor. In Michigan, for example, wildlife managers have set aside areas on public land for "treatment" (cutting for wildlife) and have the areas clearly marked. They distribute cutting permits and the locals move in en masse with chainsaws and pickup trucks, ready to do what maybe the game department couldn't afford to do—take down the trees to create wildlife habitat.

The chainsaw, then, is the tool for creating grouse cover and woodcock haunts and is also the tool of beating the power companies to the punch. However, there are some tips. First off, remember that the wood you cut is also going to have to be carried. Oak sounds great if you buy it split and stacked in your garage from a commercial cutter, but for cutting and carrying yourself, remember that, pound-for-pound, nearly all woods burn with the same amount of heat.

A pound of aspen—our favorite tree—gives as much heat as a pound of oak. I burn aspen almost exclusively because mainly I'm too lazy to grunt and groan over an oak log that needs the wedge and I hate to carry heavy logs.

Cutting aspen also creates the cover, as mentioned above, and this is where the plan comes in. If a group of wood burners can get together, and they can find some suitable wood for cutting, such as on the old deer club, they can determine how much total wood is needed for their collective need in a year. Once that amount has been figured, they can sally forth, armed to the teeth with instruments of tree demise, and cut down that amount in a parametered area. Next year, the same thing, and the next and so forth. Pretty soon, they have some good rotational cutting going on for grouse and woodcock management, and they also have their firewood.

The energy crunch has had other, more broad-reaching

effects than firewood collection. Many areas are considering wood-fired electrical plants for producing power for use by an industry or for sale to private homeowners.

Essentially, all electricity is produced by heat. Nuclear energy aside, the common electrical plants use flame to heat water to make steam to shoot at a turbine to turn a generator so the lights come on in Aunt Minerva's condominium.

The flame is usually burning fuel oil, natural gas or coal. But, oil and gas being what they are—scarce—more attention is being paid to wood as a fuel source.

Many companies are buying the wood rights to land and are harvesting the trees for use in these plants. This wood is almost always taken in what is called "whole-tree harvesting." In this operation, the whole tree is snipped off with something resembling giant scissors, dragged to a machine that chips the wood up, branches and all, and the chips are fed to the hungry furnaces. For grouse and woodcock hunters, this really couldn't be better.

Whole-tree harvesting has made large areas open to harvesting, and has made wood harvesting economically feasible to the powers that be. Also, whole-tree chipping removes the "slash," dead and discarded limbs not taken in conventional "logs only" harvesting. This slash is a prime cause of predation on young grouse chicks. About the time that the new growth of aspen comes up, and Momma Grouse leads her young 'uns into this area, the predators tag along for the meal. The slash, being horizontal, hides the horizontal line of the fox or skunk or house cat, and predation losses are high. The absence of slash makes for vertical lines of the regenerating trees, and a horizontal line (like a predator's body) is easy to spot.

The essence of grouse management is to make it easy for the grouse to dodge predators. In other words, to manage for grouse you must manage against predators. Removing the sheltering slash harms the chances of those that would eat grouse.

So far as can be determined, removal of slash poses no problems in the matter of nutrient loss to the soil because the trees are taken at a time of year when they are not leafed out. Leaves hold most of the nutrients in a tree, and these are returned to the soil as they drop in autumn and decay to be used by the tree to grow. On good soils, whole-tree harvesting apparently causes no problem.

If companies are instructed in how to do the clear-cutting so that grouse and woodcock will benefit, such as in small clear-cuts, with 20 acres about maximum, then the future of grouse looks great. But, how to get the word out?

I'd like to offer one answer to that problem—The Ruffed Grouse Society.

This organization, present and active in 17 states and Canada, was founded in 1961 by a group of grouse hunters who were troubled by the lack of grouse. They wanted some answers. Twenty years later, many of the answers have been found, and the group continues to grow and seek new answers.

The deterioration of habitat—such as aging forests—is something the Society fights with educational programs and research. Today, anything worth knowing about ruffed grouse and woodcock is part of the Society's interest. The problem of providing habitat for grouse is approached from a multifaceted angle by the group.

First off, research is a prime ingredient. Through university forestry and wildlife departments, the Society funds over $70,000 a year in research projects aimed at understanding better grouse and woodcock habits and the type of management that makes them thrive. Gordon Gullion of the University of Minnesota is the chief researcher. His projects at Mil Lacs and Cloquet, Minnesota are the standard for all grouse management today by wildlife managers.

Others, such as Gardiner Bump of New York, and Steve Licinsky of Pennsylvania, both legendary in the field of grouse and woodcock management, are part of the Society's Projects Committee which must approve all funding for the projects.

Once material and data have been gathered, the Society's staff of field biologists—men with wildlife and forestry backgrounds—use the knowledge to help individuals and industry plan their wood harvesting methods so as to benefit wildlife. The Society is almost unique among wildlife organizations because it fights nobody—it just fights ignorance. Executive Director, Dr. Samuel R. Pursglove, Jr., has taken the Society to the point that advice and counsel is sought by states when grouse are being introduced, such as in Arkansas and Missouri, and companies and corporations depend heavily on the data gathered from Society research to plan for wildlife along with the profit motive.

For example, strip mining for coal is a dirty word to many people because a strip mine is ugly. However, the Society has funded projects which will find the answers to what species of plants will provide wildlife cover quickly when planted on strip mine sites after the machines move out. The companies get the coal, Americans get their electricity from the coal, the grouse get their cover, and we shooters get our grouse—all quite quickly, I might add.

Taking the word to the private landowner is another way the Society functions. Landowners' workshops are held periodically across grouse range by the Society's field men. At each workshop, a presentation is given by a biologist—perhaps Gullion himself—on ruffed grouse life history and needs.

This is followed by a presentation by a wildlife manager on how to manage for grouse—cutting rotations and so forth—which is followed by a talk by a forester on what it's likely to cost and whether a fella can make a buck doing it by selling wood. Then, it's into a bus and an afternoon trip to an area where grouse management has been carried out so that the landowners can actually see the results.

The Society, of late, has also gotten into the educational business with children. Plans are on the board for an educational program to go into schools and outdoor education centers that will show how small block clear-cutting helps wildlife, and how species must be managed. It's good to know that the Society is fighting for grouse and grouse hunters on so many fronts.

The organization is funded by private donations, membership fees, the sale of a yearly stamp and print (a work of art commissioned and sold annually) and the proceeds of fund-raising banquets which are very nice affairs for a grouser to attend and maybe win a new 20-gauge.

The chapters of the Society—over 40 at latest tally—enjoy the opportunity to get together at their whim, talking about grouse, maybe have a grouse dog competition, invite in a speaker, have a shooting contest or picnic, and generally have a good time with others of our ilk.

If I had about 25 to 40 acres of land and I wanted to manage it for grouse and woodcock, and I didn't know how, I'd call the Ruffed Grouse Society in Coraopolis, Pennsylvania and ask for some free help and advice. I'd be glad I did, too.

In all, the topic of grouse and woodcock management is a tough subject to cover because the data is still coming in. I've presented a brief sketch, and given a suggestion about where to go for help. I'd like to refer the reader to some books, also. *The Ruffed Grouse,* by Gardiner Bump, et al, is the standard in the field. Gullion is presently doing a book through the University of Minnesota which promises to be the equal to Bump's earlier work. In addition, a booklet entitled *Improving Your Forested Lands for Ruffed Grouse,* by Gullion is available for a nominal fee from the Ruffed Grouse Society.

Steve Smith

Tailfeathers

My wife is forever hollering at me to do something with my gunning clothes—by which she means that she's sick and tired of having them scattered all over the house shedding feathers and chips of mud and handfuls of seeds and twigs and the odd shell or so. It's not that I'm the neatest person around—I don't claim to be—but I get a great deal of satisfaction knowing that I've got a hunting coat here and a pair of boots there where I can see them. And, furthermore, I've got the dogs on my side. They like to sleep on my hunting stuff, and how can they do that if everything is always hung up somewhere?

Women don't understand these things: They just see the surface and you come off being sloppy instead of thoughtful and logical. They don't understand that hunting clothes have to be broken in and they have to acquire a certain character that combines an air of rustic comfort with a certain amount of dash.

They don't understand that a man would just as soon show up naked at a hunting camp as he would show up wearing a new set of stuff. I just want my pants patched—not ironed. You can look at a man's hunting clothes and tell right away what kind of a guy he is. You can look at a man's hunting clothes and tell what kind of a day you're in for when you're going gunning with him.

I arrived in Connecticut last fall for a couple of days of grouse hunting with Dick Baldwin, who works for Remington. I was dressed like an illustration from William Harnden Foster's *New England Grouse Shooting*—tweed cap, fairly respectable shirt, reasonably good britches and a relatively new pair of leather-topped rubbers.

I must say I presented a decent picture of the "gentleman shooter." At least I could walk into a bar and they wouldn't lock the cash register. Baldwin, my host, guide and long-time friend, didn't say anything after surveying me from top to toe, but I suspect he was relieved that I wasn't affecting a necktie. (Not that I hadn't considered it.)

Dick, to say the least, was a contrast. He was dressed like an extra in a movie about starving Welsh coal miners. He wore what vaguely was reminiscent of what had once been a sweatshirt under one of those old, inch-thick canvas hunting coats. He had on a pair of hunting pants that, years past, had been faced with something the manufacturer had surely advertised as "indestructible." The manufacturer was wrong.

His 12-inch rubber boots were laceless and you could see his socks through the cuts. An old New York Yankee baseball hat was pulled down over his eyes. As we piled into the car he remarked, "I go through two or three of these outfits a year in these covers." My heart sank at the thought of what lay in wait for me, and I wasn't the least bit disappointed.

I'm sure you're acquainted with the popular illustrations and the traditional watercolors of New England partridge shooting. In the foreground are the beautiful crimson-and-pumpkin-colored maple trees. Scattered about are thinly-bunched birches, and the overall impression is a gentle rolling meadow dotted here and there with tinting trees. So much for the popular conception of grouse covers. Real, Dick-Baldwin-type grouse covers are vast, impenetrable, five-acre-sized clumps of briars, six-inch-thick grapevines and scrub oak. All this is studded with rocks that are too high to step over unless it's a bog swamp with the hummock placed nine inches farther apart than you can step. Somehow this vegetation and mire is always hunted on a forty-five-degree slant upward. (I don't know how you can hunt for two days and never walk downhill, but Baldwin knows.)

A famous historian once wrote, "Experience gives men

the ability to act with foresight." He was absolutely right. Next time my hunting partner shows up dressed anywhere near the way Baldwin does I'm going to reach into the trunk of my car and pull out a cane I now carry for exactly those moments, murmur a few words of apology about my old football knee and limp slowly toward the nearest bar.

Gene Hill

Equipment and Clothing

A visitor to some place like Dodge City, Kansas, in the last century would have seen a throng of cowhands milling around a favorite watering hole such as the Long Branch Saloon. The thing this visitor may have noticed right off is that all of these men would have appeared dressed pretty much the same. The reason is that they did much the same type of work on the great trail drives, and had developed a manner of dress which took into consideration all factors of weather, comfort, and protection.

So it has become with grouse and woodcock hunters. Over the decades, the sport hunter has developed a wardrobe of shooting dress which makes for comfort, mobility, warmth, and function. In addition, I have noticed that many such shooters, myself included, I guess, have taken a certain amount of pride in the way we look when we go afield. It's a lot easier to get permission to hunt a new cover if you don't have the remains of some long deceased grouse drying on your trousers, and the tears in your coat aren't allowing dog whistles to drop out on the back porch steps.

There are those who even affect a necktie when gunning their birds, and I have no quarrel with this. However, a tie is a bit constraining while trying to keep your head down on a right-to-left screamer well out there.

Starting at the bottom up, the shooter should take care of his feet or the day and perhaps the season can be a bust. I used to like the traditional rubber-bottom leather-topped boots for coping with the alder swales and creek bottoms. However, I now much prefer all leather, lightweight boots because of their greater support. I simply take my chances on getting wet, and carry a spare pair of boots in the vehicle with me.

The trousers can be of several types. I used to wear the type with cotton duck or light canvas material construction faced with some type of nylon or leather facing, but gave these up as they proved too hot for early season going. I still keep a pair for December gunning of grouse, but instead prefer light chino type khaki material pants sporting bellows pockets for holding all my junk.

Since such pants have no inherent protection built in, I carry a pair of those birdshooter chaps that fasten on like hip-boots and protect the legs from thigh to ankle. When these are in place, they still allow adequate air circulation and so you stay cool, yet they protect well. In the covers, you're likely to spend a lot of time bleeding if you don't take care.

Pants such as bluejeans are really too tight in the knees to allow the high leg-lifting that the bird hunter will do each day, and so they are out. In addition, these have a tendency toward too much warmth in the early season.

A shirt that is light, perhaps all cotton, in the early days of the season, will protect the arms and allow movement, but if it's thick enough to turn briars, it's probably too hot to be comfortable. In early season gunning, you'll either be hot or bloody, so take your pick. Most pick hot.

Later on in the year, a wool, flannel, chamois, or some other heavy material shirt can be substituted for greater warmth and protection. However, in the early going, you'll end up sweating and swearing most days.

Over the shirt, the gunner usually chooses a shooting vest of some type. This sleeveless item is usually the type made specifically for upland shooting as opposed to the skeet or trap shooter's vest, or an old hunting coat with the sleeves cut off.

Such a vest should have a large area of blaze orange on it, especially on the shoulder and back area. In many states, this is law, but even if it isn't where you gun, it's still smart. First off, the color is naturally highly visible, which allows another shooter to see you quickly. When gunning with a partner, this allows him to know exactly where you are so he may not have to pass up an uncertain shot. A hat made from this material is also helpful. Hats, as discussed in an earlier chapter, should not interfere with shooting.

The vest should have the snaps removed and replaced with zippers. The snaps never hold up, and buttons are clumsy. Zippers work well, they last, and they completely seal the pocket so you aren't losing shells and other stuff.

Inside those pockets, I like to carry a compass, a check-cord for the dog, and a pair of surgical forceps to take care of the quills from the odd porcupine the dog may decide to tackle, although I've never had to use them.

I've had to use the compass, though. Especially when hiking in to new covers, or hunting a big one where I can get turned around easily. I'm not proud, nor am I a blood relative to D. Boone of Kentucky and points west. If I get lost, I use the compass with no apologies.

I also carry any permission slips I'll need to hunt private property in my wallet, but the vest holds my shooting gloves when I head for the covers in the morning. I use a very thin glove on my left, or non-trigger hand, substituting a thicker one later on as things get colder. Warmth, however, is not the problem. I carry my gun pointed up, and turn brush with my gloved left hand, so I need protection here. A golf glove works well in the early season, and you only have to buy one instead of a pair.

The choice of vehicles you use is purely up to you. I use a four-wheel-drive Jeep, only because I've got one. I see no reason why a station wagon or pickup wouldn't work just as well, and the family sedan does just dandy. Most grouse and woodcock covers don't need a tank to get to, and if they do, get out and walk. Probably the biggest consideration, these days, is how much it costs to put gas into the thing. I've seen two shooters and a dog pile out of a foreign subcompact, so the choice is up to you.

But, when considering vehicles, consider the dogs. I hate

seeing a dog in the trunk or in a rear of the wagon cage. I like to have the mutt sitting in my lap, smearing the glass with his nose, and watching him eye each potential cover we pass. I also don't mind a wet dog asleep with his head on my lap for the ride home. It is part of the game.

Remember to pack a jug of water and a dish for the dog, because early season hunting is usually dry work. The dog inhales a lot of drying pollen and dust in a day's hunt, and needs a drink now and again.

In the Jeep, I carry my gun from cover to cover in a thick case of canvas with a flannel lining. Such cases allow moisture to evaporate, thus preventing rust. They also prevent scratches to the finish, but they aren't any protection against heavy objects. I have a friend who chastises me because I'm always worried about something heavy slamming down on my barrels and bending them. It can happen, especially if you toss a gun into a car trunk to rattle around with a spare tire and other junk, so be careful.

Because I fall down in creeks a lot, I've learned to carry a few dry items of clothing, such as boots, socks, and a dry shirt. If I'm a long way from home, I'll slip on the dry socks and a pair of moccasins for the drive home, and the shirt and boots can be changed at the midday lunch break if the going has been wet. Waterproofed pants usually don't need changing, unless you fell into a beaver pond.

My maps are carried in a case stowed under a front seat. I use these often, so I like to keep them handy. A netting hanging from the ceiling to hold and cool bagged birds is nice, but I haven't got around to stringing one up yet.

Shooting glasses should always be worn in the covers. Amber lenses allow you to see a bird quickly by heightening contrast between brown bird and brown background, but they get a bit bright on sunny days, so I switch to rose-colored tint. The key here is eye protection. A snapping twig or thorn can blind an eye, or can so irritate it that the day's good sport is lost in the stream of tears and squinting that lasts for hours. If you, like me, don't normally wear glasses, get a pair of shooting glasses and learn to shoot with them at the skeet or trap range. After awhile, you'll feel nervous and lost without them.

As far as other equipment goes, I'm not going to try to tell you what type of things you should have with you at all times. Certainly if you think you're going to get cold or wet, come prepared. Some of the best shooting I've had for grouse and 'cock has been when it was raining and even spitting snow. Once, Sutton and I moved a large number of woodcock in an October snowstorm. The birds never landed to be moved again, but the ones that we missed (nearly all) kept right on going. They must have figured that as long as they were up and the weather was lousy, why not keep moving? By the way, this was in the late afternoon, just when they'd be moving anyway.

What I'd like to do is discuss the things that can make the hunt more enjoyable. I've about had it with trying to get a decent meal in a roadside diner, and I get sick of bologna and cheese from a corner grocery, don't you? If so, try taking your own goodies and making a production of lunch. Grouse and woodcock shooting can be fast all day, but usually the morning and evening hours are the best, so use the two or three hours in the afternoon to get ready for the late-in-the-day shooting. Pack yourself a real lunch. Maybe some cold roast beef, chicken, cold breast of woodcock, some potato salad, or even bring along a portable grill and some steaks or hamburg. Find a nice shady spot under a flaming maple, and have a feast. Then, when you and your partner are filled to groaning, stretch out under the sheltering branches of that maple and take a nap. You'll refresh yourself for the hours ahead, and your dogs will enjoy the chance to snooze. Then, when late afternoon temperatures hold the moisture close to the ground and make scenting better, both you and the dogs will be ready. One word of caution. I've heard of fellows doing this and waking in pitch darkness. Seems they got carried away with the nap thing.

Along with all the other diaries and records you may wish to keep, none is quite so warm, and meaningful as the photographic record. Take some advice, and get a camera and take it with you on the hunt.

A simple 35mm with automatic exposure control can be purchased for under $100, and all you have to do is load the film, focus on the subject, and shoot. With the automatic eye in the gadget, F stops are automatically computed, and if shooting at a fairly fast speed, such as one 250th of a second, almost all action is frozen. You'll want pictures of friends, dogs, favorite spots, and unusual things you may find in the cover, like a hornet's nest the size of a basketball, or a picture of your buddy after he emerges from a flop in the creek. Use color slide film because the prints can be made from this, and in slide form, it's fun to invite your pals over after the season, settle back with a little Jack Daniel's and switch on the slide projector for a nostalgic trip to past seasons. This also works as a panacea during the heat of the summer, when the gunning season is weeks away, but you know in your bones, that it should start tomorrow. This whets the appetite a bit, as well as forestalling the crazies.

Other Trophies

A great many grouse and woodcock shooters have started to collect other types of things related to the sport as a way of adding to their pleasure of this way of life. Many collect limited edition prints having to do with shooting and the sport, and are justly proud of their collections. So popular are these items, that fund-raising banquets for grouse and woodcock organizations almost always feature an auction or raffle for a limited edition print, and the finer sporting catalogs carry them, framed or unframed.

In addition, many carvings of grouse and woodcock are presently hitting the market. A good one is not cheap, but it is as much a work of art and source of enjoyment as a fine sculpture.

Having a bird or two mounted by a reliable and competent taxidermist is also a good way of dressing up the place in the house where you keep your hunting gear. Luckily, a grouse or woodcock mount is not as expensive as having, say, a deer head and shoulder mount done, and they can be displayed on a table or desk to add to the flavor of the place. A lawyer of my acquaintance has his law offices decorated in early ruffed grouse. Shooting prints adorn the walls of each office, and several excellent mounts are displayed throughout his spacious place of business.

I like to keep and display the tail fans of all ruffed grouse I shoot as a kind of trophy or memento. I do this by taking the tail off during skinning, and spreading the fan out. I sprinkle the connecting meat liberally with salt, and fan the tail open and cover it with a heavy weight, such as a large book. After a week or two, it will keep this position, and I tack it to a piece of rustic looking barnwood, covering the salted meat end of the fan with leather and some tacks. I add a little notation below it telling where and when I shot a particular bird. A glance at this board at the end of the season gives me a lot of satisfaction. A glance at the display about midsummer gets my blood boiling to be gone hunting.

Many fine pieces of literature exist on grouse and woodcock shooting, and the public library and book clubs offer these for loan or to buy respectively. However, many shooters pride themselves on their sporting collections, and they look in all kinds of out-of-the way places to pick up original editions of such works.

Many companies are now reprinting some of the classics in the field to sell to a new generation of gunners, and I'm one of the first to have my check there for my copy. Reading grouse and woodcock prose is a fine way to pass the summer nights before the season opens.

Steve Smith

Why

O nce in a great while, when my wife shames me into it, we have a little party at the house. Invariably some meddling woman will notice the all-too-few woodcock shooting prints I have hanging on the wall or the all-too-few decoys in my sketchy collection. "You shoot *birds?* How *can* you?" And then I try to explain to her the difference between the swing-through method, the pointing-out method and maintained lead. If that doesn't confuse her out of any further remarks, she can be counted on to say "Oh I don't mean that. I mean how *could* you? The defenseless little things . . ." Mentioning the fact that she is wearing a leopard skin coat that was probably poached by some African with a poisoned arrow, has absolutely no relation to the conversation. Save your breath. *Birds* are different.

It's of no help either to try to explain the ecology of so much land—so many birds. It does no good to explain about nature's law of the survival of the fittest; or that she's just knocked back second helpings of Pheasant Fricassee; or to point out that without the restraining laws of nature and predation etc., etc., she'd be up to her sweet derrière in bobwhite quail or wild turkey.

What she wants to know—or have you admit, is that you are one hell of a killer, teeming with blood lust, who comes home from a few hours in a meadow or marsh with enough stiff game slung over your bloody shoulder to pull the rivets on your truss.

This, for some reason *I* don't understand, *she* understands and will accept as a perfectly valid reason. A friend of mine who makes his living, more or less, by working, more or less, for a gun company, is by nature a big game hunter. His answer as to why his house is decorated from cellar to attic with heads of antelope, impala and the outer garments of lion and leopard and zebra, is guaranteed to stop the nonsense. He merely smiles a very mysterious smile that I'm sure he's practiced over African campfires, and says "Oh, I guess I just like to hear the thud of bullets smack against some solid flesh."

But what happens when you ask yourself the very same question? Some excellent recent anthropology, notably Robert Ardrey's fine book *African Genesis*, claims that man owes his evolution to the fact that he learned how to kill. Ardrey has satisfactory evidence that man's first tools were killing instruments.

Maybe we kill just to keep our hand in, in case the job folds and we lose the mortgage and end up back in the father-in-law's cave.

The non-hunter doesn't understand why you and I can go out and swamp it all day long, not popping a cap or cutting a feather and be delighted, if not satisfied, with a nothing-to-nothing tie.

I guess I don't really believe that hunting is a *sport*. I tend to agree with Hemingway who said something to the effect that only mountain climbing, bull fighting and automobile racing were sports and that everything else was a game.

To me sport entails some grave element of risk. And hunting so rarely involves danger—not counting stupidity—that it doesn't qualify.

So let's say that hunting is neither a game nor sport. Trap and skeet are games and delightful, but hunting is a thing apart. It requires some involvement.

A lot of deep thinkers claim that hunting is largely a sexual thing. I won't or can't argue that. I tend pretty much to agree, but hunting has more than sexual undertones.

I think each of us understands it in his own way. You hunt for your reasons and I hunt for mine. And each of us is satisfied in his own way.

I think I hunt because I'm afraid of death and shooting is to me a very deep and complex way of understanding it and making me less afraid or more reconciled to my inevitable end.

I think I hunt because I envy wildlife and by having this control over their life is to share in it.

And I think I hunt because I have been hunted.

I know I hunt without regret, without apology and without the ability to really know why. Let's say I get a sense of satisfaction out of it that stretches back to the beginning of man's mind. I hunt because I am a man.

We are still young animals ourselves. Chronologically speaking we are only hours old compared to the birds, the fishes, and the bug that lays us out with flu.

We hunters share some ancestor wrapped in stinking robes of skin who would greatly envy us our three dram load of 8s as he stares at the polished shin bone of an antelope he holds cocked and balanced in his hand.

As the dog has the ancestral wolf, we have the ancestral killer too, tucked away, and not too deep, inside.

Gene Hill

Book design by:
Remo Duchi